C000155682

and ANOTHER thing...

First published in Great Britain in 2004
by Artnik
341b Queenstown Road
London SW8 4LH
UK

© Artnik 2004

All rights reserved. No part of this publication may be reproduced, stored in or introduced into a retrieval system, or transmitted in any form or by any means (electronic, mechanical, photocopying, recording or otherwise) without the prior written permission of both the copyright owner and the publisher of this book.

ISBN 1 903906 45 8

Illustration: Martin Rowson
Design: Mark Lloyd

Printed and bound in Spain by Cayfosa

and ANOTHER thing...

THE BOOK OF RANTS

ARTNIK

The Obsessive-Delusional Ranter (definition)

These people can't turn it off. They fixate on everything, and **need** to talk about it. These are the people you have to find an excuse to walk away from because they just won't shut the hell up. They have an opinion on everything, whether they know anything about it or not.

Their websites – hardcore ranters always have a website – are unfocused, blindly-meandering blather fests that may start on one topic and end up passing through twenty new topics before finally ending in a non sequitur or some comment about a failed love affair two years ago.

They'll talk about the oatmeal they had for breakfast and come up with four reasons not to talk to chipmunks on a weekday and then get started on their opinions about Jewish headwear...all in the same log entry. They are severely agitated personalities who hunger constantly to express all the myriad thoughts in their head, but often have no one to listen to them.

These people need a pre-frontal lobotomy followed by a cinderblock head message, before being put on a diamorphine drip and a hookah packed with *Purple Haze* skunk.

Anon

CONTENTS

Calumny is only the noise of madmen.

Most men are within a finger's breadth of being mad.

Diogenes, 410 – 320 BC

Introduction

A rant is both an expression of our frustration at the state of the world and an acknowledgment of our impotence to change it. King Lear's rant against the elements is a defining example of the form – a bitterly disillusioned and enraged old man shakes his fists at the sky, daring the weather to do its worst as it soaks him to the bone. As if the weather's actually *listening*...

But we, the audience, are. And while his rant is utterly pointless we identify with his defiance and, most of all, appreciate the way he expresses it. When the ranter rages at some aspect of the world, he is not doing it to change things but to make his point and, more importantly, make it with some wit and style. A rant, even when it is written, is often a kind of street theatre – it's the stand-up routine of the man in the street or, in case of *And Another Thing's* prototype ranter, the London cabbie.

A lot of London taxi drivers treat their cab like Diogenes did his tub - a platform to go off about everything and nothing. When Artnik asked me to compile 'The book of rants', I knew that London's black cab drivers would provide me with some of my best material. I hope that you, the reader, agree that they did.

There were other quite unexpected sources. Celebrities always make the most obvious hate figures for hacks and anonymous members of the public alike. Yet I was pleasantly surprised to discover that some celebs can tub-thump with the best of them. Who'd have thought that Julia Roberts would take a career-damaging swipe at her own government? Or that Kurt Cobain reserved a fair portion of his considerable bile for Jean Claude Van Damme? If *And Another Thing...* proves anything, it is that *everyone* hates or loathes or despises someone.

One particularly obvious aspect of the rant's uselessness is evident in the anonymity of several that I have selected for this book.For all the focused rage and occasional eloquence on display, many ranters don't really want to stand behind their rants. It's almost as if they know they'll regret it all later, but it feels so wonderful to get it off their chests. The Internet has been an unprecedented breeding ground for the committed ranter, who can fire off his or her most vitriolic soundbites without fear of reprisal or regret. 'Full of sound and fury, signifying nothing...'

Rants are a crucial part of a free society, however. They are democracy red in tooth and claw. They are how people get it off their chest, have their say, make their point…and that is their whole point. They are freedom of speech in the making.

And another thing… if some born-again health counsellor tells you that ranting is not good for you and that you really ought to go on an anger management course, tell him/her/it that Diogenes lived till he was ninety.

And Another Thing… was edited by a group of Oxford graduates who had a riotous time compiling the book, learning cabbie-speak and spectacularly failing the 'Knowledge'.

Artnik would also like to thank the many Internet ranters who permitted us to use their material. Where we have edited their material (often for legal reasons), we have tried to remain true to the spirit of the original.

1

The trouble nowadays is everyone thinks they're a celebrity

LONDON CABBIE on Victoria Beckham

And another thing...that Victoria Beckham. She's everywhere. Magazines, papers, ads, Parky, you can't even watch an England game without 'em showing her in the crowd. I mean who does she *fink* she is?

Posh! She's about as posh as Battersea Dogs' Home, which is probably where she came from.

All she is is David Beckham's wife. The only thing she's ever done is marry him and his money. Got to give her credit there. Like he's so rich he can afford to hire a ghostwriter to write his text messages. You know those text messages he sent to his genuine bit of posh – that whatsit's name bird of his...Loos? He didn't write them. No way. You've only got to hear him talk to know that. He can't talk two words together, never mind write 'em.

But at least Loos is real. That Victoria is more plastic than Jordan. Every time you see her there is something different about her. She's been having nip 'n' tuck big time. And what about the boobs? They're looking more like balloons on a stick insect...

Don't get me wrong, Becks is a good footballer – not great mind you, *good*. Set pieces there is no one better in the world. Well, except when it comes to penalties. He don't like it when it's one-on-one with no wall in-between. But football is more than just kicking a dead ball and Beckham, let's face it, is a bit of a one-kick pony 'cos he can't do much else. Sure, he can whip those crosses in but that don't make a play-maker. 'cos Zinedine Zedane he ain't...no pace, can't tackle, can't head.

That's why he has run into trouble at Real, they've put him in the middle of the park and his brain ain't up to it. He is not the quickest of thinkers, is he? He can't be, can he? Otherwise he would never have married her.

AMANDA PLATELL on Victoria Beckham:
Daily Mail

She's as fake as her tan, as brittle as her acrylic nails. My first reaction on hearing that David Beckham may have been playing away with his former PA Rebecca Loos was, who could blame the poor soul? And I was not alone.

If every woman in the country who felt even a shred of sympathy for Victoria gave a tenner, there'd be just about enough to buy a handbag from TopShop.

I'm afraid the truth is that from the moment she burst upon the pop world as the least talented, yet most ambitious member of the Spice Girls, Victoria has been anathema to women.

The trouble nowadays is everyone thinks they're a celebrity

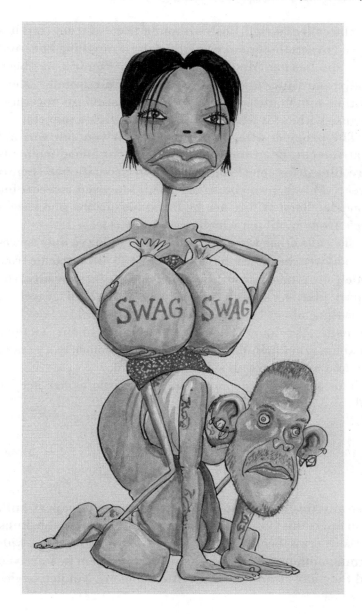

She called herself Posh without a trace of irony and has proved over subsequent years that she is anything but. And since she became Mrs David Beckham, Victoria has been totally parasitic upon his fame. It's no wonder she's fighting tooth and nail to keep this marriage together, because without it what is she? A faded, failed pop star.

The problem with Victoria was what you saw was not what you got. Even their most intimate 'at home' moments were filmed for television, usually to promote her singing career. This is a woman so desperate she used a recording of her husband telling her he loved her on the phone in a single from an album which is yet to be released.

She calls other women 'cows' and in doing so only serves to reinforce her own bovine qualities. As a female role model, she is past parody; as a model of physical beauty, she is past plastic. Victoria is greedy, grafting and graceless. Everything about her is fake – the tan, the breasts, the lips, the nails, the hair. The only real thing about Victoria Beckham is her ambition. And that's why women can't stand her, and why we are all siding with David.

That girl had it coming. She's as brittle as her acrylic nails and about as Posh, too.

Posh
Summer of George:justramit.co.uk

Basically this comes down to petty spite...the papers built them up as this 'fairytale' couple, knowing full well it stuck in their craw because they were two working class kids earning millions. Now the chance to bite them has arrived and they have leapt on them with malicious, vindictive glee and they try to drag the public in to give the whole sordid charade a wafer thin facade of public concern.

She was in the Spice Girls. She was s**t. She launched a solo career…it was s**t. It failed, as it deserved to, but she continued to work on it. So this meant she didn't move lock and stock over to Spain when he did, and this is the reason he started shagging around. 'It's her fault…' I'm sorry, run that by me again. 'Her fault for not going to Madrid with him.' What century are we in?

These are the same harpie journalists who are quite happy to drivel out long fawning articles about '20 ways to be go-getting modern women'.

The vitriol that has been poured on her…can't these journalists write each other poison pen letters instead?

Male Celebrity C**k of the year
Summer of George:justramit.co.uk

Always a tightly fought battle for this prestigious award, so many to choose from…so few winners.

Jamie Oliver – fat-lipped celebrity chef and professional scooter twat, for his sterling work in bothering to exist.

Garry Bushell – hardy perennial and regular attendee of the COTY awards, generally doesn't leave empty handed – good old fat impotent racist.

Jeffery Archer – over privileged ponce, sadly not nearly gang-raped enough during his stay in a luxurious holiday camp masquerading as a prison. Proof enough that even the nation's criminals shun this f****r.

Chris Evans – ohh, you unemployed spoilt ginger twat, lost millions of pounds…pretending it doesn't bother you…I bet you w**k yourself to sleep every night over your *Big Issue*.

Richard Littlejohn – ahhh dear Dickie, mouthpiece of the far right and not at all obsessed with the sight of grown men thrusting, pounding their hard glistening man-meat into each other in wild abandon in any article that he bothers to write.

'We are proud to announce this year's winner, despite stiff competition, is Richard Littlec**k.' (Many thanks you neo-fascist hack.)

Female Celebrity Strap-on of the year.

To show the lovely ladies that they too can be rewarded for behaving like screeching harpies as well.

Julie Burchill – fat, unfunny, bitter, old hag with a laughable squeaky voice and no idea what she is talking about. Welcome back after missing out so closely last year.

Cherie Blair – letter-box mouthed Mekon look-alike who, as well as being a QC and property wheeler-dealer has managed to grab every freebie holiday or gift that she could get her shovel-like hands on. Carole Caplin has done wonders helping her to stretch her mouth into something a toad would croak on.

Amanda Holden – vapid little troll who automatically gets a nomination for wanting to sleep with Neil Morrissey and Les Dennis when not heavily medicated. Add to that her general sluttish behaviour and her lack of talent and she is a strong contender...oh, and she's obviously a hopeless gold digger to boot.

Clare Sweeney – aggggh, loathsome bint, her work in Brookside was so bad it deserves a special JustRamIt award of it's own but now she seems to think she is some kind of f*****g singer to boot.

'The winner – *yes I can still go windsurfing or lie on the sofa moaning Jam Rags* – goes to Julie Burchill.'
(Julie, 73, based in Bright-on-charlie-town, is waddling onto the stage as we speak, viewers of a particularly nervous disposition should duck for cover now.)
Me (helium voice) *Julie Burchill, I am wonderful, my father was working class and I used to be thin. My genius as a writer is in the way I can be so shocking and yet compassionate too...*
'Thank you Julie... Let's bring back the birch for Julie folks. I'm sure you'll agree seeing her in the flesh is even more proof of why we should never buy any magazine or newspaper that pays her.'

A quick rundown of the other unmentionable C**ks and Strap-ons.   **Best Female Newcomer:**

Jade Goody – walrus faced monster, clubbed to death live on air as part of our Sky Sports sponsorship deal.

The award for the person whom we would rather eat the contents of a litter tray than meet goes to **Naomi Campbell** who, even when she is not snorting charlie in the Priory, is amazingly stupider than anyone could imagine.

International Idiot TV star of the year goes to **Kim Bauer** – the bit of nubile totty on *Rocking 24* who manages to get in more scrapes than a slutty Penelope Pitstop drunk in Ibiza.

Finally let's honour our C**k On the Block Lifetime achievement award for deflowering barely-legal pole-dancers.
'Hear it for **Mr Peter *Pedo* Stringfellow**...' (A rousing chorus of farmyard noises greets *Pedo* as he climbs onto the stage shaking his luxurious mane, his face looking like a distressed Zelda from *Terrahawks*.)
'Ladies and Gentlemen, we are proud to announce that due to service to being a C**k above and beyond the call of Duty we have decided to honour Peter *Pedo* **String-him-up-fellow**. We all swooned in awe as he launched a women's perfume last year called Lapdancer which managed to incorporate the haunting mixture of scents and aromas which hang so seductively in the air of his nightclub **String-him-up-fellows**. A delicate blend of smoke, vomit and sweaty G-strings mix delightfully with the pungent aftertaste of smegma...'

We at JustRamIt would like to say thank you *Pedo* for coming up with the perfect Christmas present for our mum. We wish you the very best in whatever scheme your addled, senile brain comes up with next, especially if it is an elaborate suicide plan.

www.filmrot.com on Michael Winner

Yeah, just look at Michael Winner. Winner never got a chance to go down hill in his career – he started at the bottom and never budged...

CLARE MCKEON on Gwyneth Paltrow
The Sunday Mirror

Gwyneth Paltrow has become very irritating. The multi-millionaire says she cannot understand why women put their careers before children.

I suppose it wouldn't dawn on the little peewee brain that some people have to earn their money and don't have the luxury of choosing to be or indeed of being full time mothers even if they really want to be.

There is nothing worse than an overpaid Hollywood bore lecturing and pontificating to the little people. She knows absolutely nothing and seems to be divorced from reality.

Last week she spent 1,500 euros in a week on a chauffeur to pick up hot macrobiotic meals made by her team of three chefs to deliver them to her on the set of her latest movie.

Gwyneth go away and leaves us alone.

KURT COBAIN on Jean-Claude Van Damme

He said, 'Yes, Larry [as in chatshow host Larry King], when we were shooting the film we found the indigenous people of Alaska to be some of the most warm, friendly blah blah blah etc.' Another retarded action adventure side of beef longing to portray himself as a distinguished actor. His PR man transcribed a basic English 101 course on a piece of paper and Jean Clod Goddammne actor man must have studied the answers to the harrowing questions for at least a week. Now that's entertainment.

Watching Sylvester Stallone fumble his way through an interview with that Yo Duh Fred Flintstone accent while spewing out sentences that maybe, uh, a really smart guy might say, with a lot of 'as well as', 'pertaining to' etc., blah.

The indigenous people of Alaska? What are you f****ing talking about? The Eskimos? Or the drunken redneck settlers who never see sunshine who are up to their ballsacks with raw dead fish guts on a boat for nine months out of the year?

PETRONELLA WYATT on Non-Brits in London
The Spectator

I think we should institute two new annual awards. The first would be entitled 'The most infuriating non-Brit in London' prize.

There are an embarrassment of candidates. Mad mullahs, would-be suicide bombers, Madonna, who has reinvented herself as often and to as little effect as Marks & Spencer, and a host of other irritating immigrants.

But were the first award to be bestowed this year it must surely go to Gwyneth Paltrow. She has pointless good looks without sex appeal and is relatively pointless as an actress.

Miss Paltrow, who moved to London to live with her British husband, has now started to criticise London. Doesn't Miss Paltrow know that it is bad etiquette for anyone but Londoners to complain about London? It is our privilege to criticise the rain and traffic wardens and black taxis, not that of visiting American celebrities. Miss Paltrow's conduct is that of a guest at a dinner party who moans loudly about the food, the dining-room and the hostess.

The other annual award I would institute is for the most infuriating pregnant woman: the woman who speaks most volubly about the awfulness of gaining weight.

Speaking as someone who often attempts diets – and finds them extremely incompatible – I would be only too glad to have the excuse to eat pasta, bread, chocolate and other fattening foods; as, I suspect, would most women. These include the millions of women who go through tortures trying to conceive a child or those who can't conceive at all.

Perhaps plastic surgeons should pioneer a new service to really silly women – pregnancy liposuction. Your stomach reduced with no ill effects.

Numerous celebrity culprits regail us with details of their pregnancies. I do not want to hear such details any more than I want to learn about their lavatorial habits.

ALUN PALMER on Double-Barrelled Names
The Mirror

There is something about women with double-barrelled names on television. That extra moniker adds so much more gravitas than their mere presence on our screens, after years of boarding and finishing schools, it should make us eternally grateful.

Added to the list of the likes of Vicki Butler-Henderson and Tara Palmer-Tomkinson is Nicky Hambleton-Jones.

If her name isn't sufficiently irritating, her voice is enough to have cats and dogs wincing in pain.

In *Ten Years Younger*, not only did she mangle the English language but she strangled it at birth.

Coupled with a voice like fingernails scraping down a blackboard, she had the demeanour of a priggish school ma'am with a class of naughty eight-year-olds.

Nicky Clarke gave her a haircut and a dentist gave her a new set of teeth. Then a plastic surgeon was unleashed to pump her so full of Botox that when she smiled it stayed put for a couple of decades. The eyebrows were plucked and she was given a new wardrobe, all costing a remarkable £7,500 – well within the reach of most Channel 4 viewers.

Nicky may have been a Tory MP's dream come true, but she is to presenting what Antony Worrall Thompson is to haute couture.

TERENCE BLACKER on Madonna
The Express

Madonna bought a chunk of Britain so she could play the part of a country toff. But she is behaving like a spoilt brat.

First she complained about low-flying aircraft and then erected a security gate without planning permission. Now she is fighting tooth-and-nail to keep ramblers off her estate.

Madonna likes our land but resents our rules. If she craves privacy that much she should go back to the States – where she can buy it.

OLIVER JAMES on Boring Celebrities
The Mirror

At its simplest, the likes of Edwina Currie, the late Alan Clark MP or actor Richard E Grant differ from us in their self-importance.

They believe that because they are shagging the next prime minister (as Currie was), fancying the present one (Clark had the hots for Maggie Thatcher) or rushing to Madonna's house for dinner, the hoi poloi will want to hear about it. They also think we care what they think.

Diarists are often people who live behind a mask of falsehood. No real emotions are expressed to others. Deep down, that leaves them feeling desperately lacking in simple human contact.

The only person with whom they feel they can have an honest exchange at the end of the day, literally, is themselves.

DAVID THOMAS on George Michael
Daily Mail

George Michael has earned tens of millions of pounds over the 20-odd years since he first sent teenyboppers screaming as one half (in truth, the half that had all the talent) of Wham!

With homes in Hampstead, Highgate, Regent's Park,

Berkshire, St Tropez and Texas, he certainly doesn't need any more than the vast amounts he's already got.

George Michael may be a highly intelligent, articulate and charming man, but he is possessed of a smugness, bogus piety and near genius for twisting reality to suit his own perspective.

The ultimate example of this gift for spin came after his arrest for 'lewd conduct' in a public toilet at the Will Rogers Memorial Park in Hollywood, California.

When Hugh Grant was caught in a comparably embarrassing position with a female prostitute, he promptly embarked on a coast-to-coast marathon of public apologies for his degrading behaviour.

George Michael was rather different. He conducted an oleaginous TV interview with Michael Parkinson, the content of which was prearranged at a lunch at an exclusive London restaurant.

Now he's moved on to a new image – the idealistic millionaire hippy who just wants to give his art to the people. Perhaps it's just the drugs talking.

George freely admits to smoking cannabis like other people sip glasses of wine.

He's cut back recently, he says. He's down to four joints a day. Oh, and the occasional ecstasy tablet, for special occasions. Perhaps that explains his latest eccentricity – or maybe it's something else. George Michael turned 40 last summer. He's lost his appeal to the teen market and has yet to capture older listeners.

He likes to pretend that this is a blessing in disguise. Asked recently to name the worst thing about being George Michael, he replied: 'That my fame is irreversible.' Actually, it's very reversible indeed, and George knows it.

JIM MCBETH in *The Scotsman*
The Beckhams

My contemplation on abstract matters, which impinge on the reality of my unique place in time and space and history, continued when I found myself wondering what some people are for. Like Posh 'n' Becks.

This is a big subject and you will no doubt have your own opinions. But they appear a couple whose lives are defined by a strange (stupid) dynamic, hard for Normals to comprehend.

Consider...the media is bursting with David Beckham's alleged infidelity. Now, this is a defining moment in his life and the future of his marriage.

Mr Beckham naturally denies any impropriety and runs to his wife, to explain.

Victoria is a former Spice Girl. Now, they are in a hotel room. What do they talk about? 'Darling, I love only you' or 'I have been faithful to you since the day I first laid eyes on you' or 'Don't believe that crap in the *Sun*'?

No, they talk about clothes, about choosing complementary matching outfits, a marital ensemble with which to meet the Press.

Not just that they play dress dollies with their youngest wean, presenting him to the world with his new ear-ring. He's a child, for God's sake.

What were they thinking about? I know Becks and Vickie sound dim, but can they be so crassly daft? Well, yes, they can. Am I alone in believing that we are becoming more stupid as a society?

I don't just mean the stupidity of the Beckhams, but that of afternoon television interviewers, such as the demonic

Richard & Judy, with their insensitive bovine detritus.

Example: Richard interviewing a transsexual, who was once a man, then became a woman, and wants to revert to the masculine. 'Well,' says (the) Dick: 'Did you miss your penis, or what?'

That's television stupidity, in a class of its own, confined to the damaged world inhabited by the likes of Jordan and Peter 'I'm an arse, get me out of here' Andre.

You can turn it off, but you cannot turn off life and the idiocy is spreading to the non-celebrity brain dead.

It is insidious and difficult to escape.

Take some shop assistants and telephone receptionists. Please take them.

CASSANDRA (Bill Connor) on Liberace
the Daily Mirror [26 September 1956]

He is the summit of sex, the pinnacle of masculine, feminine and neuter, everything that he, she and it can ever want.

I spoke to sad but kindly men on this newspaper who have met every celebrity arriving from the United States for the past 30 years. They all say that this deadly, winking, sniggering, snuggling, chromium-plated, scent-impregnated, luminous, quivering, giggling, fruit-flavoured, mincing, ice-covered heap of mother love has had the biggest reception and impact on London since Charlie Chaplin arrived at the same station, Waterloo, on Sept 12, 1921.

This appalling man, and I use the word appalling in no other than its true sense of terrifying, has hit this country in a way that is as violent as Churchill receiving the cheers on VE day.

He reeks with emetic language that can only make grown men long for a quiet corner, an aspidistra, a handkerchief and the old heave-ho. Without doubt he is the biggest sentimental vomit of all time. Slobbering over his mother, winking at his brother and counting the cash at every second, this superb piece of calculating candy-floss has an answer for every situation.

Nobody since Aimee Semple McPherson has purveyed a bigger, richer and more varied slagheap of lilac-covered hokum. Nobody anywhere ever made so much money out of high-speed piano-playing with the ghost of Chopin gibbering at every note.

[Liberace sued the Mirror for suggesting that he was homosexual – something he vehemently denied right up to his death, when the truth was revealed. The jury awarded him £8,000.]

MARGO MACDONALD on the The Wessexes
Edinburgh Evening News

Wow! Sophie and Edward network as part of their work in the media...him in TV, her in PR. Well, blow me, that's surely taking unfair advantage of meeting all those people, from every walk of life, and from every business sector, in the course of their royal duties.

You'd hardly credit it but Prince Edward, on being shown round the spectacular gardens of the Sultan of Brunei during a royal visit to promote all things British, mentioned his real job was in TV programme-making and, if the Sultan was interested, his company would love to make one about his garden. He probably gave him a business card, too.

I mean, why do Edward and Sophie need to earn money? Couldn't they just get money from the Government to open things, visit places to schmooze for Britain and live exemplary lives? No? Then how should they support themselves? Should they just freeload off the Queen?

Suppose they packed in the titles and made themselves unavailable for trips like the one to Brunei. Would that allow them to behave like his mother's other subjects in their personal and business lives without being set up by news-papers 'in the public interest'?

Unlikely.

For all the criticism, an awful lot of people still like the idea of real royals showing up to do what royals do...giving occasions a touch of importance and class.

Of course, it's not strictly necessary for the hoi-poloi to rubberneck at a royal for some presidents and their families fulfil the same function.

The same proved true for Bill Clinton. Americans wanted to believe he had only a simple zipper problem. That he was a proven liar didn't fit the profile they had constructed for their first family.

It wasn't until he wouldn't leave the stage gracefully, that he got the media treatment meted out to the House of Windsor every day.

Monarchy or republic? In terms of how we, the people, react to the personalities made and unmade by the media, there's no difference.

JIM MALLON on *The Passion of the Christ*
Internet

Perhaps those engaged in the moral/theological discussion over Gibson's 'The Passion' ought to take a look at EBay's site devoted to the film. Ads there suggest that Gibson has seen fit to license souvenirs to promote the film, such as a crucifixion nail necklace (sans blood but with a reassuring quote from Isaiah). Other EBay items: a Jesus Christ hip flask (which a friend noted brings new meaning to the phrase, 'Christ, I need a drink') and, my personal favourite, a Jesus Christ money clip (Pharisees notwithstanding, do you suppose the Lord would carry 10s, 20s or 100s as his 'walking-around money'?).

That his film is controversial is undeniable, but Gibson's licensing of tasteless merchandise robs him of any moral high ground in the debate over the merits of the movie. How much money is this man making off the crucifixion of Jesus Christ?

VICTOR LEWIS-SMITH on TV celebrity chefs

Despite being a restaurant critic of many years standing (why the waiters won't ever let me have a chair is something I've never understood), I'm not particularly fussy about food. I want my steak rare, and I *mean* rare ('just knock off its horns. wipe its arse, and bung it on the plate garçon'). And I want my shellfish to be large and well-cooked, or else I'm straight off to the small clams court. But having eaten far and wide in this country, I can tell you that the oft-repeated statement that 'British food has never been so good' is garbage, because over the years, I've had almost as many dreadful gastronomic experiences as I've had hot dinners. Throughout this land, I've eaten sausages that have been nothing more than condoms filled with sawdust, the piece of cod that passeth all understanding, and roadkill in a bun served on a tablecloth so filthy that it looked as though it had recently passed through a Yogi's digestive tract, during his quest for inner cleanliness.

So contrary to the *im*propaganda churned out by innumerable tv food programmes, we do *not* have the best cuisine in the world. No, in truth, we're home to some of the worst food on the entire planet, yet the British food industry boasts of its culinary excellence to such an extent that it doesn't just take the biscuit, it takes the entire Nabisco Factory. Surely with a national dish that consists of tasteless fish and fatty chips, and a national drink of warm beer that enters and leaves the body in exactly the same condition, you'd think we'd show a little humility? But if we do, then I'm a Dutchman.

Chez Vjiktor Van Lewis-Schmidt, the expression 'TV Celebrity Chef' has been banned, because television has played a large part in the destruction of gastronomy in the UK. Its juvenile obsession with turning every branch of human endeavour (from music to antiques) into a competitive sport has debased the art of good cooking by turning it into a game show, with celebrity chefs taking us into new realms of pointless infantilism as they reduce gastronomy to a branch of light entertainment, despite frequently possessing only a wafer-thin knowledge of the subject they claim to excel in. No wonder my French friends (one of whom is a three-star Michelin chef) tell me that when they come here and switch on their TV sets, they

The trouble nowadays is everyone thinks they're a celebrity

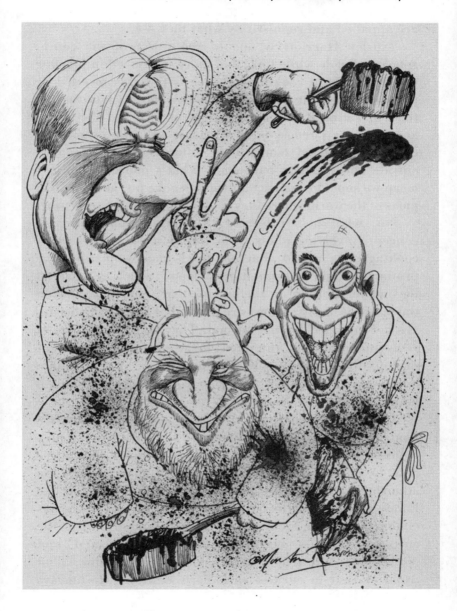

are appalled and repulsed by what they see.

Ainsley Harriott is one of the worst of the genre, spookin' for de white folk, and more interested in juggling the food than in cooking it (which is fair, because I'd be more interested in throwing what he concocts into the bin than in eating it). Or he's telling us that we should all abandon our purpose-built kitchens, and our ovens with carefully-regulated temperature controls, and instead go outside and learn to barbeque. What's more, he doesn't mean we should construct a proper smoke pit, as they do in parts of the world where they *really* know about barbecuing.

No, what he's referring to is a peculiarly British concept, involving idiots from Basildon who believe that cooking on a naked charcoal fire somehow justifies the production and consumption of food which is charred beyond recognition on the outside and salmonella-raw on the inside. Ainsley's shows are proof that British barbecues are not intended for the normal. They're really a form of Darwinian culling, intended to weed out the sort of profoundly stupid people who pour cans of petrol onto bonfires 'to get it going', and then wonder why they end up looking like Simon Weston.

It wasn't always this way. There was a time when TV food programmes existed simply to improve the nation's culinary skills, with the likes of Fanny Cradock showing us how to mix a perfect batter, while Johnny looked on admiringly and told us 'I hope all your donuts turn out like Fanny's.' But over the past fifteen years, the emphasis has changed from education to entertainment, with the culinary formats becoming ever more absurd and irrelevant to the true requirements of fine cuisine. That trend started in earnest with Fern Britton (who always looks as though she's got two dwarves wrestling beneath her jumper), and her dreadful *Ready Steady Cook*. As host, she constantly encouraged bun fights and other games with food, which is why the studio soon came to resemble nothing so much as the 70s kids' hit *Runaround* with vegetables (or 'presenters' as I believe they're officially called).

Even those who try to pass themselves off as serious TV chefs are required to debase themselves by cultivating an increasingly eccentric image, in order to attract the commissioning editor's eye. Think of the rotund Antonio Carluccio turning himself into a wildly-gesticulating parody of an Italian, doing some weightlifting for the cameras (or 'standing up' as everyone else calls), and talking endlessly about mushrooms, even though he's not a fungi to be with. Or Gary Rhodes, a potentially fine chef who can't help basting his ego in the warmth of the cathode rays, and always seeming convinced that *he* is the dish of the day. Tragi-comically, so does Antony Worrall Thompson, forever winking at the lens in the mistaken belief that he's something of a ladies' man, when in reality he looks increasingly like one of those plastic pigs you see outside butcher's shops. And the *Two Fat Ladies* had to adopt the dodgy personae of a pair of fake 'eccentrics' to get their big break, perched unconvincingly atop their vintage British motorcycle, which was the only Triumph in an otherwise appalling show. Until, that is, the Grim Reaper intervened and turned the double act into the far less objectionable pairing of One Fat Lady and One Small Urn.

In recent years, programmes have ventured still further downward, descending from the zabaglione of light entertainment froth into the seedy world of gastroporn.

Nigella Lawson is the Linda Lovelace of this genre, of course, a once prim-and-proper woman who (once she'd discovered that Diamonds are *not* forever) suddenly began cultivating a new image as a sex goddess whose every movement now seems marinated in erotic overtones. Her way of eating strings of melted cheese is the gastroporn equivalent of the 'money shot', while her obsession with stuffing citrus fruits up the rear ends of chickens has been rivalled only by Sherlock Holmes. Well, surely you remember the meerschaum-smoking sleuth once describing this process as 'lemon entry, my dear Watson'?

Saddest of all are those potentially superb chefs who sell their sole to the media, in return for a ticket on the media gravy train (all aboard, chew chew). I'm thinking here particularly of Jamie Sainsbury (né Oliver), who was refreshingly innocent and full of genuine enthusiasm for his art when he first hit our screens. So much so that, after his first programme, I sent him a fax saying 'Congratulations. Just keep doing what you're doing, and keep doing it with integrity.' But then I added, 'because if one day I see your f***ing face on a saucepan, I'll know you've sold out and I'll headbutt you...' This shows once more that my words are valued by the world at large at about a halfpenny a ton, but then again, the path to hell is paved with food intentions.

Can there ever be integrity in food programmes nowadays? Of course. Nigel Slater and Delia Smith have both managed to get inside the magic rectangle without jettisoning their integrity, and to get out again when they had nothing more to say. In both cases, they wanted to showcase their cooking, not their egos. They know that the place for one's personality to sparkle is at the dinner table, whereas solid advice and quiet expertise are what's required in the kitchen, the sort of advice that three-star Michelin chef Christian Willert once gave to me when I was staying at the wonderful Palme d'Or, at the Martinez in Cannes. 'If you're inviting people over for *le Weekend*,' he told me, 'remember that fish and guests go off after three days.'

Who's to blame for the increasingly nasty taste that most TV food shows leave in the viewer's mouth? J'accuse the fearsomely heterosexual Peter Bazalgette, because the downward trend began with his wretched Bazal Productions company, and its lamentable eighties flagship, *Food and Drink*. During the nineties, he introduced the 'cooking against the clock' format, which has done more to debase and vulgarise TV gastronomy than anything else. It's curious that the Bazalgette family first achieved prominence through their sterling work with drains and sewage, and fitting that Peter is keeping the family connection in place by smearing our screens with excrement.

Great cooking is a time-consuming blend of art and science, creating esculent masterpieces that can only truly be savoured and appreciated in a restaurant, not a TV studio. Why? Because a single complex dish often requires many different cooking processes to come to a climax simultaneously, and that's a feat that can only be achieved by an experienced and skillful team, working together in perfect synchronisation. Chefs who love their art know this, which is why many of the greatest names in gastronomy are virtually unheard of outside of their own profession; they refuse to fritter away their time and their talent for the benefit of TV cameras, and know that, if you *can* stand the heat, then you shouldn't get out of the kitchen.

Alright. Perhaps this sounds a trifle harsh, but before sitting down to write, I'd just spent an hour attempting to make Provençal grand aioli, and it ended up looking like a bowlful of snot, so I'm not in the greatest mood. But one thing is beyond doubt. Far too many intelligent and basically decent chefs have allowed themselves to be seduced by the lure of the lens, and have ended up by abandoning the serious pursuit of their profession altogether, in favour of joining the ranks of the 'celebrity chef'. But as they do so, they should remember one thing. Celebrity is the mask that eats away the face, and that's ultimately a very grim feast indeed.

GORDON RAMSAY on Antony Worrall Thompson

(I don't really get him. Thompson keeps on saying that I am bad for the industry – I don't know why. I didn't f*** off to the jungle with a thong up my arse and sit there asking for my agent did I?

So let Antony continue launching his latest organic yoghurts with his beautiful face on the side and his ginger beard and let me f***ing cook. I don't give a f*** what he or anyone thinks about how I am – I'm just showing the industry for what it is without any f***ing airs and graces.

ANTONY WORRALL THOMPSON on Gordon Ramsay

This is the man who phoned me up and said, 'God I'm so jealous of you going on "I'm A Celebrity". I'd have loved to do it but my father-in-law, who looks after my finances, wouldn't let me.'

He also said his wife really likes me and he thinks I'm a good chef and let's go out for dinner and sort things out. Now he's slagging me off again. He's a hypocrite.

It may be that I have to sue at some point. My lawyer says, 'We can get him if you want.' I could have sued him twice but didn't. He will get me to the point where I will have to take legal action. He says very slanderous things about me that could be detrimental to my career, like me not being able to cook or not encouraging young chefs, both of which are untrue.

The problem with Gordon is he's always slagging off me and Ainsley and the other TV chefs, but he refuses to admit he's a TV chef as well. I can only think he's jealous of me really because I have restaurants as well as a successful TV career. I know for a fact he went for auditions early on in his career because we have the same agent.

VICTOR LEWIS SMITH on TV Hypocrisy
Evening Standard

And we welcome viewers now to the final stages of the 2004 100 Greatest Moments of TV Hypocrisy awards.

Ex-Marxist Alexei Sayle is still at number three for doing voiceovers for banks, while in at number two is anti-bullying campaigner Craig Charles, who once threatened to push me 'straight through a plate-glass window' after I'd reviewed one of his programmes.

But this year, the judges (me) have decided there can only be one winner: Gordon Ramsay, who used to berate celebrity chefs for demeaning their art, but has now turned into the PT Barnum of gastronomy, force-feeding his audience with rancid entertainment that's hard to swallow.

Gordon Ramsay rants :'My job is not swanning around the customers' tables in a starched apron and starched Y-fronts. Customers don't want to see chefs at their tables but they love coming into the kitchen.

'I have one group of eight female lawyers who regularly blow their money on a bloody good dinner at my restaurant. They always come into the kitchen afterwards and hang around. Eventually, I have to ask them to go back to their table. They say: 'We'll only go back if you tell us all to f*** off.'

What's that all about?

JOAN COLLINS on the EU
Independent on Sunday

Why should anyone regard Joan Collins as a key voice in the Britain and Europe debate? More than half her life in Hollywood, fading (faded?) celebrity, a string of second-rate movies behind her, a preference for the south of France, and yet she purports to speak for England. She is emphatic about that: England, not Britain. If you were conducting the great debate would you call on the Queen of *Hello!*?

'Beware of the euro! Even lemons cost more since the single currency came to St Tropez.' As political slogans go, hardly designed to catch the floating voter. 'I know what I'm talking about,' wrote Joan, 'as I have a house near St Tropez and, since the French adopted the euro last year, the cost of running it has risen by nearly 30 per cent.'

Last Sunday, incredibly, Joan was back. This time in the *Sunday Times*, occupying two-thirds of a page headlined 'They're trying to kill my England'.

This time on the EU constitution. 'I have an apartment in New York and a house in the south of France,' wrote Joan, undermining her credentials to speak for England. But speak she did, at ignorant and hysterical length.

Look out for the next Collins rant.
The Express version cannot be far away.

JOHN MCVICAR on *SIR* Cliff Richard
Artnik

When Hurricane Ivan was rampaging across the Carribean, I prayed — and I'm a hard-line atheist — that it would rip into Barbados. It didn't, which was further evidence of the futility of looking, however desperate you are, to the skygods for help.

I've never been to Barbados, I've nothing against Bajans... in fact, I don't even know any. BUT there is a former plantation on the island called Sugar Hill that 'has a fantastic view of the sea, cooled by gentle breezes and with an amazing tropical garden'. David Lloyd, former British Davies Cup captain, who talent-spotted Tim Henman as a 10-year-old, developed it into a luxury residential estate with coralstone villas. *Sir* Cliff Richard owns one.

For the last two years, the Blairs have stayed in *Sir* CR's villa. They rather like the vulgar chic of ruched knicker blinds, fake silver chandeliers and gold lions, but Tony especially likes the tennis court. He would, as he has been playing since he was coached as a youngster at his private school. What Tony doesn't like about playing CR, though, is that he has to let our Peter Pan of Pop win.

Now Tony has been driving me mad from virtually after he came into office. The first few days I was as pleased as the rest of us, but then I discovered that all those people who spontaneously came out to line the Mall and Downing Street to wave little Union Jacks as he made his triumphant entrance to No 10 had been recruited by Alastair Campbell. It was a stage-managed, completely phoney event. I never really recovered.

My Phoney-Tony condition, though, is manageable. The wife monitors my blood pressure and once it climbs above 140/100 she allows me access only to the sports pages, stops me listening to R4's *Today* and watching *Newsnight*. There were difficulties during Tony's delusions about Weapons of Mass Destruction — I couldn't stop myself tuning in behind her back and the BP went 180/140. But the doctor prescribed satins (reductase inhibitors)...

Cliff Richard is a different kettle of fish. For forty year, he has been gradually turning me psychotic. *Only Sixteen... Summer Holiday... Congratulations... Living Doll...* and, that mother of all diarrhoea, *Millennium Prayer*. His syphilitic musical spirochaetes enter, feed off and propagate in my brain...

The psychiatrist told me to protect myself against further infection by doing everything possible to insulate myself from his records. There is also the medication but, even with it, there have been some full-on Jack *The Shining* incidents. Thankfully the wife has lived to tell the tale... and does she like to tell it when we have guests for supper.

However, then came my own personal 9/11. It was a rainy July 3 1996. I was at my computer and the phone rang. A friend...well up to then I always thought of him as so, but what he did revealed him as a bubonic rat crossed with a cockroach.

He knew about my *Sir* CR condition and how vulnerable I was to any untoward exposure. He asked, 'Are you watching?'

'What?' I replied.

'Wimbledon! You've *got* to put it on.'

I said that it's raining...there's no play. 'No. I *mean* it. You've got to put it on. You'll never believe it.'

I shrugged and said, 'Alright', put the phone down and switched on BBC2...

With a microphone, *Sir* CR was singing to the centre-court with a back-up group of five lesbians tennis players. *Singing in the Rain.* If the word gobsmacked was coined for anything it was this moment, but the brain's synapses couldn't handle this overload from hell. My brain spasmed then, as its cells combusted, everything just froze. Catatonia. It saved me from some ghastly convulsive seizure but it meant I couldn't shut out this Boschian, Dante-esque vision. The wife found me, and the men in white coats did their best...

It's torture living inside a twisted, warped, diseased brain, yet there was one compensation. I suddenly discovered I'd become one of those retards who are geniuses in just one area, like being spastic but an incredible musician, too. My idiot savant gift was I could see right through the conspiracies.

Now some conspiracy theorists think that it's the Jews or the Zionists or the Masons or Ron Hubbard or Bill Gates who are behind it all. But they are wrong. I know who's behind it all...well in this country anyway.

And it's not Tony Blair. Why do you think he can't beat CR at tennis? Younger, better player...he's tanking because he knows who's the boss. In Blighty, it's our Popsicle of Pop who's behind it all. Behind Henmania, for instance. It's no coincidence that David Lloyd, who built *Sir* CR's villa in Barbados where the Blairs stay, *discovered* Tim Henman. *Sir* CR never misses a Henman match at Wimbledon. *Never*. He created Henmania. Why? Because it's only Henmaniacs who'd buy his revolting records.

It's the same with the Millennium Dome. Who do you think was behind that monstrosity? Who sang *Millenium Prayer*? Think what it looks like from the sky. That dome is *Sir* CR mooning for Jesus...

It all makes sense once you put it all together.

Our born-again Christian who found Jesus at a Billy Graham revivalist meeting, who forswore sex to do God's work, which is why he never married (not even Sue Barker), who would never proposition a cop in an LA lavatory, who set-up his own Wimbledon singalong...is behind it all. Behind New Labour, the Nanny State, Political Correctness...behind anything that dumbs down the plebs enough for them to tolerate his execrable music.

This is why, if Hurricane Ivan had answered my prayers and obliterated *Sir* CR from the face of this earth, I wouldn't have felt guilty about a few Bajans going with him, especially if Tony got caught in the backwash.

2

All due respect, there's some people...

NICKY HASLAM on Being Common

It's nothing to do with class, money or background. It's an instinctive thing. You just know when something is common – it's coarse, old-fashioned, outdated and vulgar. It is always about making your life more difficult and less lovely.

I mean jet lag was fine when aeroplanes were first invented but we've all got used to them now. Get over it, for God's sake. And talking about being ill is the worst. Nobody wants to know.

Being ex-directory is common. Why have a telephone if people can't get hold of your number? Cuff links are common. My friend Hardy Amies thinks that they are ageing and he is right. Buttons are much nicer and more modern. Yellow dogs are common and so is water. People seem obsessed with this common little drink.

I think the sun is a bit passé too, not the tabloid, but that hot thing in the sky.

It's common to make people go outside and smoke. I have a friend who had just been through rehab and about the only thing she had left in life were a couple of little ciggies. She asked this pathetic little duke whom she was having dinner with if she could have a cigarette and he said no. She got her revenge. She asked him to dinner and, when he said 'What about a drink?', she replied, 'Oh terribly sorry but we don't drink here.'

Dancing on your own, especially at nightclubs, is terminally common, and so are showy weddings in grand houses that have no connection with your family. Crude best man speeches that expose the sexual peccadilloes of the bride and bridegroom are also frightful, and so is clapping in the church.

Going to the gym is vain and self-centred and very common, and so is using party as a verb as in 'we were partying all night'. Young people smoking cigars is inelegant, silly and common. They think they look cool but they don't – and they make such a thing of it.

I think all this nonsense about food is common. My favourite food is white bread and cheese slices.

I think the whole class system in England is a nightmare. The new aristocracy are the young rock stars and designers.

A MISOGYNIST on Women
Artnik

The thing about women is that they are all, without exception, quite mad.

This is not a sexist generalisation. This is cold, hard

scientific fact. Please don't misunderstand me, I love women. No man who has been married as many times as I have could be called a misogynist. No, I simply understand that while they appear to be governed by the same laws as the rest of us, in fact they occupy an entirely separate world. One abstracted from rational behaviour. One where it is perfectly acceptable to burst into tears for no reason. One where they expect people to understand them when they say the exact opposite of what they mean.

It's possible that you know a woman who you think is sane. Perhaps you've only just started seeing her and you're still in the first flush of love. She's yet to make a scene when you suggest meeting your friends for a drink. She's yet to throw a strop when you compliment her on her dinner. She's yet to throw anything at all, in fact. But it's only a matter of time: trust me on this. You'll say the wrong thing when she's trying on her fifth outfit of the evening. And there's no way to avoid saying the wrong thing, because there are no rules that govern their reactions, and no logical relationship between stimulus and response. That is what we mean by madness.

Many of my best friends are women. But I would not vouch for their sanity, and I would never trust them with my happiness.

FREDDIE WINDSOR on Mobiles at Wimbledon
Artnik

I don't know if you've ever been lucky enough, as I have, to watch a Wimbledon tennis match on Centre Court. If you have in recent years, your match will almost certainly have been interrupted at least once by the chirruping of a mobile phone. Usually, the sound is not especially loud and is cut short straight away. However, occasionally it actually starts off quietly and then becomes louder, culminating in a horrible computerised squawk that coincides with its hapless owner discovering it at the bottom of her handbag. When this happens, it inevitably throws the player's concentration and, since mobiles became widespread about eight years ago, a number of crucial points have gone against the receiver because of this.

It's not asking much to turn them off, but to do so nevertheless appears beyond the scope of many people's thinking. If you consider that a mobile goes off every five minutes somewhere in the stand, just imagine how many more must be switched on at the same time, owners oblivious to the tiny point-bombs in their pockets. I would estimate that at any given moment perhaps twenty mobiles are at risk of deciding play; it's only a matter of time before one goes off with Tim Henman, match point down, reaching for a second serve. Brring! Brring! *Clunk* as the ball hits the tape. 'Game, set and match Feddick (or whoever).' What fun that would be.

But, believe it or not, this isn't a rant about mobile phones on Centre Court. As annoying as these little interruptions can be, they are as nothing compared with what follows. Imagine the scene: it's six on a dryish first week afternoon, and the big men's singles is the third match to be played on Centre. 5-6, 30-40, second set. A phone rings. Wearily, and often for the third or fourth time today, the umpire responds:
Ladies and gentlemen, as a courtesy to the players, please ensure your mobile phones are switched off.

40

It begins slowly, almost apologetically but, within seconds about half of Centre Court, a good five thousand people, are clapping as if appreciating a brilliant passing shot. Like almost nothing else at Wimbledon, this boils my blood. It strikes me as an extension of that maddening sheep syndrome that we all remember from school assembly: a inquiry is made and, once one hand goes up fifty others swiftly follow. The maddening holier-than-thouness, the oily I-agree-with-Sirness of it.

Once I recall watching one such do-gooder gloriously betrayed mid-clap, as a jarring version of *Rule Britannia* sliced through his breast pocket and sent him into paroxysms of embarrassment.

Nowadays when I see umpires about to make such an appeal I bury my head in my hands and hum – it's my way of not hearing all the sheep bleating their approval. Why don't they just bring in football rattles or learn anti-mobile chants to spring on everyone after the umpire has spoken? That would at least be more interesting than the current situation. Spare a thought, too, for the umpire; how embarrassing to be applauded simply for stating a basic point of court etiquette.

I suppose my main problem with these third-form sneaks is that their behaviour makes me really want more phones to go off, just because I know it will upset them.

TINA BAKER on Pavement Terrorists

He's cute, but younger than me. He has nice eyes. He's dressed casually, as if to say 'Hey, I don't need to try too hard.' He has a beautiful smile. And, thanks to some miracle, (Thank you, thank you, thank you, God!) he's beaming it my way. I suck in my stomachs (three at the last count). Our eyes meet, engage, flicker into possible futures. But, just for a second, I glance down. Which is when I see it. The clipboard.

Curses! Another sodding chugger!

I swerve to the right – he counters. I duck and nervously smile my 'I'm usually a kind person but I'm really busy' smile, all the while frantically searching for a gap to dash through, as he starts his dementedly enthusiastic spiel. He thrusts his hand forward for me to shake, body blocks, and pursues like a heat-seeking missile, as I do a triple-twirl, half-piked dismount off the pavement, into the path of a marauding dispatch cyclist, (don't get me started on another rant!) and escape across the road. Simultaneously he unleashes a barrage of guilt daggers into my retreating back while rugby tackling an old lady who valiantly tries to beat him off with her tartan shopping trolley.

This kind of charity harassment happens at least 17 times on my every foray to buy cat food down the local High Street. I'm now officially A Bad Person to the power of 17. Yet they – the failed drama students and phone-sales scum who make up the new breed of pavement terrorists – remain humanely immune to rejection.

So, once and for all:

Yes I have thought about it.

I already give.

I know you're on commission.

You piss off more people than you get to donate.

And you're causing an obstruction.

Now bugger off.

ANDREW MARR on Aristocrats
Daily Telegraph

The aristocrats left in public life are there because they are rumbustiously talented and no one's yet chopped their heads off (Lord Strathclyde); or half-apologetically, under demotic camouflage (Michael Ancram); or as faintly sinister plutocrats (the Duke of Westminster).

As for the rest, the old aristocracy is to be found in a condition of internal exile, lurking in rural idiocy, making jam and money from the land; preening for *Hello!*; lurching across the dance floors of farouche London nightspots or black runs in Gstaad; and running art galleries in Chelsea back streets. It's hardly the Red Terror, but nor does it add up to a serious role in British public life.

I really cannot see that more dukes and Old Etonians are the answer to Britain's democratic illness.

RUPERT CHRISTIANSEN on Country house opera
Daily Telegraph

Let's be brutally honest here: for all our egalitarian pieties, there's still a secret thrill about being admitted to something grand, foreign, expensive and sold out.

The unabashed playing of this card is one reason for the current boom in country-house opera.

Yet this pastoral entertainment inspires an astonishing amount of puritanical vitriol. Nothing seems to bring the simmering class-hatred that infects our cultural attitudes to the boil faster than the thought of people paying a lot of money to get out their gladrags, listen to unamplified music and eat a picnic. It's a ritual that seems to hit a raw nerve in the liberal press, provoking babble about the evil of toffs, snobs and elitists in dinner jackets, popping champagne corks and plotting counter-revolution.

ROGER MARSH on Youth Culture
The Times

I am a busy person so I tend to eat as, when, and where I need to and I do not feel that I am breaking any age-old protocols in doing so.

However, I do agree that there is a massive decline in overall standards and this, in my view, has been very much driven by youth culture or, more appropriately, the lack of it.

As a youth, I was loud, obnoxious, wore ridiculous clothes and had my hair in a variety of macabre styles and made a deliberate attempt to look and be different from everybody else. I did not, however, spit, swear, spray graffiti, vandalise (ad nauseam) or create litter, and I generally respected figures of authority.

Today's youth do all of those things (and more) and have created a culture of their own because of it.

Some of this behaviour has undeniably spread to older, middle-class people – there's nothing sadder than seeing a 40-year-old wearing expensive trainers, tracksuit top and bottoms (all designer labels, of course), a checked baseball hat and sporting bling to boot! Then, as if they are not ridiculous enough already, they open their mouths and spew out a string of expletives and a few grunts which pass for conversation these days.

PENNY MORTIMER on Charlie Whelan
Sunday Telegraph

My temperature rose a notch or two more last Saturday when I read an interview with Charlie Whelan (ex-spin doctor) on his new career as a fly-fisherman.

He maintains that, until now, fly-fishing has been mostly the sport of toffs, far above the price range of non-toffs. For a start, who or what is a toff? The dictionary says it's a slang word for someone who is well dressed. Well, it's OK to be well dressed, isn't it? I mean, even Tones wears Armani, darling.

No, I think Charlie Whelan probably means 'person with money'. I'm not sure how much money you must have to be a toff (are Posh 'n' Becks toffs?). Anyway, it's a silly word that smacks of class hatred and brings to mind the contorted, angry, ugly face of John Prescott in mid-rant.

TAKI on Jade Jagger
The Spectator

When Marlene Dietrich heard Richard Burton and Elizabeth Taylor complain they were fed up with staying in hotels blockaded by fans, she advised them to stay in ones where she wasn't staying at the time. The Kraut, as Ernest Hemingway always called her, knew how to tell publicity seekers a la Taylor where to get off. I thought of Marlene a couple of weeks ago, when some jeweller flew in Jade Jagger and boyfriend privately (that's as in a private plane) in order to publicise her wares.

Luckily I never saw the wretched couple – she looking

simian with an attitude to match, he dressed in a black T-shirt with hair sticking out of it – but I was told all about them. The last thing this station d'hiver needs is third-rate celebrities like Miss Jagger. Or second or first-rate, for that matter. But it's always the third and fourth-raters who make it unpleasant.

Mesmerically talent-free, Jade manages to be successful – at what I do not know. Attitude, I guess. She must have inherited this from her mother, the unspeakable self-publicist Bianca. It is difficult to describe. It is not like a duchess having smelled a fart – God only knows most of them are experts at that – but more like a faux grandeur, which the celebs, as the plebs they are, cannot pull off.

Mind you, I don't mean to be mean about Jade Jagger, a woman I have never met. But I've seen pictures of her hauteur, and it's really a no-no. Youth confuses courtesy with deference, ergo the rudeness, but she ain't as young as she used to be. Actually, it's her old lady who perfected the look, the Margaret Dumont 'how dare you speak to me' kind, and it's the last thing I wish to see here in this peaceful alpine village full of bad-tempered peasants.

No, what bothers me is that Gstaad is getting so popular with the wrong people. For one, they drive these enormous SUVs, which hog roads that are already too narrow. Recently the first Hummer arrived, with Monte Carlo plates, natch. I have not been able to see who drives this ridiculous machine, but it's surely someone with a very, very small penis.

Or with very, very big tits.

Noel Coward used to sing 'Why, oh why, do the wrong people travel?' All I do is think about why the wrong people drive the wrong cars and come to the wrong place in winter.

A LONDON CABBIE on Homosexuals

And another thing, them homosexualisers that are everywhere nowadays, what has happened to the world? As if I want to listen to music on my wireless sung by a bunch of people who like to stick their whatsits up each other's jacksies. There used to be a law against it, nowadays they make them ministers! That Peter Mandelson – wasn't he the one dressed up as a woman on Clapham Common... Alright it wasn't him but it was one of Blair's ministers. They should all be sent back to Greece where it began.

Lesbians I understand, a bit of harmless fun and, if they're attractive and that, then it's actually quite nice. Of course the lezzers can't actually have sex with each they can just kiss and cuddle, which is okay, but not gays – horrible little men with tight tee shirts, droopy moustaches and hampsters in cages. All of them.

Of course you can't even say the word 'gay' now, it's illegal. Bloody thought police. I don't have time for them or their politically correctness, it's the nanny state gone mad, I'm used to causing a spade a spade, me. In fact I called a spade a spade the other day in the street. Stupid bastard punched me in the face.

Send 'em all back to where they came from, I say. Them...and the faggots. Back to Greece where they belong. Olympic Games, that's where it all started, you know... Not a lot of people know this about the old Games, but in those days women weren't allowed even to *watch*, never mind compete. Men only. Once you've got *all* men, it stands to reason you've got trouble...

...I had that Richard Littlejohn in the back of the cab once... *now there's a very clever man.*

47

KURT COBAIN on The Right-wing

When I think of Right Wing I think of Ronald Reagan clones as mayor in every state of the US. When I hear the term 'Right Wing' I think of Hitler and Satan and civil war. When I think of Right Wingers I think of terrorists who plot to kill and terrorize the lives of planned parenthood practionists.

The reality of getting an abortion in this country is very scarce right now due to Randall Terry and his pro-life Gestapo who gather in churches dressed in the best camouflage possible (lower-middle-class chameleon polyester from the warehouses of the home shopping network). In the House of God, Operation Rescue is a non-profit organisation plot to unveil yet another helpful household hint to helping their duty as Godfearing commonfolk...

They put nails in the driveways of clinic staff and doctors. They make never-ending threatening and violently abusive phone calls. They stand outside abortion clinics every day all day with pickets and loud, violent threatening words of wisdom from God.

These people have criminal records. They have marksmen and terrorist skills. They steal foetuses from abortion clinic dumpsters and throw them at Senators, Congressman or just about anyone who is involved in government who is a Democrat.

These people basically have the same beliefs as white supremacists who also claim to act and embrace their ideals on the grounds of GAWD. Right wing is the foulest, dirtiest insult a person could be called. These people hate minorities of all colour. They will perform mass-extermination of everything that is not white, godfearing and right wing.

R is for Republican.

BRIAN MCDERMOTT on Trains

There are few more unpleasant experiences than getting a rush-hour train on a wet day. You walk in the rain to the train station, stand on an exposed platform waiting/ praying for the arrival of a train. The first train arrives and you can't get on because its too full. You wait another five minutes and this time you squeeze your way onto a carriage. If you are wearing glasses they will immediately steam up, and you can't take them off to clean them because you are clinging onto a pole with one hand, and using the other to hold your umbrella, which is dripping onto you.

I remember hearing a politician extol the virtues of public transport, outlining the stress that drivers experience stuck in rush-hour traffic. Bad as being stuck in rush-hour traffic is, at least you endure it in a warm, dry seat, not squashed up against complete strangers.

Human beings were not meant to be that close to strangers.

TONY FITZPATRICK on Cyclists in London
TFA

Many years ago I hosted a weekend radio show on London's most popular station, LBC. After years of driving in London and having cyclists disregard any road protocol, appearing from nowhere and threatening any car driver with bicycle chains or – just kicking the side of my car – I'd had enough.

So I started the 'let's make cyclists take the test!' Road drivers pay congestion charge, are regulated through MOT, have to pass a driving test and pay exorbitant rates of insurance. What do cyclists do? They cycle through red lights as though they were irrelevant, risking injury to drivers and pedestrians alike. They have no regulation by law – have no driving test to take – and aren't insured if they cause an accident. I felt, as a law-abiding citizen – that things had to stop. Little did I know the response I was to get!!

Overwhelmingly drivers [and there were hundreds of them] were on my side. Calls came in in their droves – but so too did the 'cycling fanatics'!

I was threatened with such choice phrases as 'we know where you park' – 'the word is out on the streets – gettim!' and other such pleasantries. In the end I ended the campaign after my car had been scratched, windscreen wipers pulled off – and wing mirrors smashed!

Cyclists! Do I hate them? No! But why should any person travelling by any form of locomotion not be regulated by law and have to prove they are sufficiently capable?

By all means take to the road by cycle - it's cheaper, healthier and better for our environment. But why, when this form of transport can cause road crashes, injury or death to drivers and pedestrians – should cyclists be immune from the law?

I don't – and am not allowed, to take a short cut across a pavement, I wouldn't pass through a red light because I think there's nothing coming in the opposite direction, and I certainly wouldn't have the audacity to threaten other drivers because I feel like.

Call on a ban for unlicensed, untested cyclists. Teach them the Highway Code – and make them take out insurance. Whether you're a driver or a pedestrian [or another cyclist!] – your life is in danger. Stand up for your rights – *and make them take a test*!

CHRISTINA ODONE on The Countryside
The Guardian

Every spring, just as surely as the cuckoo will herald the new season, country people raise a fuss about their rights being abused, their environs polluted, or their neighbourhood trashed.

The countryside, we're taught in hymns, poems, and *The Archers*, is the cherished heart of the nation. In fact, the country shelters and amplifies everything that is worst about Britain. The self-image of country folk is of salt-of-the-earth types who work hard, suffer in silence, and are the backbone of the nation.

Rural Britons like to claim that theirs is a loving, tight-knit community where everyone leaves their homes and cars unlocked, and helps the old biddy across the high street. But even a brief stay in the country reveals people with a suspicious mentality who shun – and often gang up on – the 'stranger' in their midst. Blacks, Muslims, Jews...not many of whom will you find living among the meadows and hills that harbour bigots in Barbours and racists in gumboots.

Farmers' livelihoods are not guaranteed by hard toil but heavily subsidised by the very state they love to rail against. Nor have those who work on the land done much to preserve their much-vaunted beauty spots. Wander into the centre of a town or village after dark, and you will find it either dead, or overflowing with drunken yokels shouting abuse and taking part in urinating competitions.

Despite the great PR they enjoy, country folk are not terribly nice. How many times will some mule-head hog a country lane with his tractor, inching along while a queue of vehicles builds up behind him? How many toffs get away with outrageous churlishness because feudal forelock-tugging survives in the shires?

The country is also the haven of curtain-twitching curiosity. In this stagnant fishpond, everything you do is noted – from the make ('foreign!') of the new stove carried in by the delivery men to the dress ('too revealing!') you wore at the harvest festival supper.

Explain that you're gay or admit that you're a single mum and you'll be given the wide berth once reserved for lepers.

Next time the hicks from the sticks try to enlist your sympathy in their latest battle to preserve their hallowed way of life, don't lift a finger. They're not the best of Britain – they're the worst.

STEVEN BERKOFF on Women

While the great female wail is going up, just think that the road along which you casually drive your man-made, man-designed automobile was built by the sweat of male labour, and while listening to your man-made radio in your comfortable man-made leather seats, and listening mainly to male rock and roll, you then enter your man-designed, man-made building, built by male labour, get into your male-invented lift and be safely escorted to your man-made office desk, where you will switch on your male-conceived designer computer and proceed to type some journalistic drivel about the evil male!

EDWARD DE BONO on Bullying

There are few things I hate. I do not like the stupidity of arrogance. I do not like meanness of jealousy. I do not like loutish behaviour. I do not like extra loud motorcycles in city streets. But I do not hate any of them.

It's bullying I hate even though I was never really bullied. At school I was always two or three years younger than anyone in my class. This is because I skipped a class on two occasions. Instead of moving to the class above, I moved to the one above that. I was probably only bullied for about three minutes in my entire school career. The reason was I usually teamed up with the toughest boy in the class, which is one example of the way brains can always outwit brawn.

Yet there is only one name that I remember from my kindergarten days. It is the name of the 'big bully'. I wasn't one of his victims but I still knew that what he did was horrid. To enjoy attacking and tormenting someone weaker, who cannot fight back, is cruelty for its own sake. To inflict pain on another person for no other reason than the pleasure it gives one is, in fact, the first small step a child can take into evil.

There are those who while they do not condone bullying will excuse it in children as 'natural' behaviour. Nature does not inflict pain for the pleasure of it, though. A animal will kill another for food or to protect its young, not for enjoyment. Bullying is not natural. At its most extreme, when torture is done for the fun of it, it is pure evil.

This is why I hate bullying.

JOHNATHAN MARGOLIS on people who use 'Innapropriate'

Of all the crappy, weaselly, half-hearted, half-arsed, half-brained, regurgitated management-speak trash words and phrases, of all the aural faeces with which we are pelted on a daily basis ('Passion', 'Outcomes', 'Solutions', 'At this time', 'Lessons have been learned', 'Moving on', etc), one word, one rancid, greasy ball of pompous, insolent verbal spittle, stands out: 'inappropriate'. 'Inappropriate' is flung out like a life-raft twenty times a day by the dimmer kind of social work bureaucrats, patronising Blair-babe junior ministers, idiot local councillors, corporate Haitch R creeps and jobsworthy senior coppers. Apart from the actual personage of the intellectual cripples who find the need to use such a linguistic crutch, the single most annoying thing about 'Inappropriate', frustratingly enough, is that it's actually, er, inappropriate.

Inappropriate is used because the twats who burp it up are too scared, too 'inclusive', too unsure of their own pallid beliefs, too hypocritical to say something in proper English, such as 'wrong', 'bad' or 'unsuitable'. Apart from the fact that such a fancy word makes them feel big and important, the Inappropriate brigade's defence of their buzz word, of course, is the wish not to offend people or behaviours that are wrong, bad or unsuitable. The difficulty with that, sadly, is that it is they themselves who are offensive because their overweening political correctness deems them too testicularly challenged to say what they mean. They believe that by saying 'inappropriate' instead of 'wrong' that they will soften their message. In reality, those who are charged with being inappropriate simply regard their accusers as c***s.

PETER MCKAY on John Hurt and Jonathon Aitken
Daily Mail

Actor John Hurt is said to have had difficulty 'stringing a sentence together' while presenting an award to Sigourney Weaver with whom he starred 25 years ago in *Alien*.

His opening words at the Empire Film Awards ceremony at the Dorchester Hotel, London, were: 'Well, well, what a silliness.' He continued, according to a *Mail* story on Saturday: 'And what a beauty. And what a glory. To be able to stand here and introduce, and at the same time to give an award to, a woman who is extraordinary.' Perhaps Mr Hurt had been drinking before the event. Two days beforehand he had been escorted from the lapdancing club Spearmint Rhino.

Talk of the autocue machine breaking down is dismissed by a member of the production team, who says: 'There was another reason for the problem which was all too apparent.' My sympathies are with Mr Hurt.

Ex-convict Jonathan Aitken was gracious (belatedly) after Michael Howard slammed the door on him returning as a Conservative candidate. Earlier, he'd complained about dirty tricks by party officials who were against him re-applying for his old Thanet South seat.

Perhaps he should seek redemption on reality TV as the token toff on *I'm A Celebrity...* or *Big Brother*. This is now the accepted route to public acceptance for dodgy characters.

Mr Aitken possesses both low cunning and high-mindedness. He used to be (maybe he's reformed) the kind of man capable of lecturing a girl about the need for high standards in public life while spanking her. I think he'd perform well in the jungle or the *Big Brother* house.

The Continuing Television Presence of Jeremy Clarkson
Summer of George: JustRamIt.co.uk

Who is watching *Top Gear*? – Please report immediately to your nearest police station for instant lobotomies performed with a corkscrew and no anaesthetic.

Not only is he a rabid xenophobic Thatcherite twat, he also has a huge turd for a brain. This is a vital part to remember, a lot of people hate Clarkson but forget the entire s***t-for-brain factor.

Its very easy to focus on his portly vile body, saggy melted face or pathetic attempts to look young by wearing a leather Jacket.

These in themselves are all fine.

Then there is the voice: that halting use of sarcasm that never fails to warrant needles in the eye: 'We took the new Rover 500 ... [ridiculous pause]...through its paces.'

But no, It's his huge reeking crap sitting in his skull that is his real problem. Plus those who watch *Top Gear* are just the kind of assholes who buy car magazines full of soft porn shots of 'glamour models' in bikinis lying on the bonnet of a Renault Clio.

Look, if you want one of the wrist, there is plenty of hardcore filth about and DVDs can be hidden much easier from the missus – these are some of the benefits of advanced technology, new and more convenient masturbation options.

Bet they like Formula One as well – look, men changing tires on a Sunday afternoon... excuse me I have to spend the day tearing all of my body hair out with rusty tweezers so I will have to give it a miss.

Don't get me started on his slick-haired toff Sidekick, Quentin Marigold or whatever.

Kilroy was here

Well, I heard all about Mr Kilroy-Silk's recent troubles and my feelings went through a threefold rollercoaster. Initially I was outraged. I'm a firm believer in freedom of speech, then I remembered we were discussing the right of Robert Kilroy Silk to have freedom of speech and I thought, 'F*** that.'

I'm glad they took his show off. If they need a stupid Brummie to strut around, butting into peoples conversations, full of their own self-importance and with an unstoppable urge to patronise the general public, I can be available, just make the call, Auntie.

Let's be clear here, I have no interest whatsoever in what Kilroy has to say about anything, he's a cretin. His soporific show has been running for 18 years.

Unbelievable... it's awful. Bear in mind it's morning television and so is expected to be crap, but they gather a barely coherent gaggle of congenital halfwits on bleachers, and in wanders Mr Perma-tan for his intro.

Now apart from the fact that his introductions generally consist of a series of stupid questions rather than anything salient, it's a miracle this joker wasn't thrown off the box earlier.

'Have you got Fishy Hands?'

'No gag Reflex?'

'Perhaps your Grandmother makes her own prunes?'

'Kirsty from Swindon has a similar story.'

And off he rushes to some brain dead single mother with a squawking regional accent to listen to her drone on. It's not until the little caption comes up that you have the faintest idea what the show is about. Followed by the crushing disappointment when it reveals the show is about 'I lost my house due to my addiction to Scratch Cards'. Again.

Now, it's well documented that his demeanour on the show is that of a pompous arrogant dicksplash, because he is, so I won't go into his laughable presenting skills. But during the recent Brouhaha he has made a statement along the lines that he has 'learnt more about the opinions of the ordinary person while presenting my show than I ever did as an MP', and that ordinary people are tired of being gagged. This says three, nay four things to me:

1 What a p****. Obvious, I know, but had to be said, I'd pay to see him gagged, then beaten with sticks.

2 It exposes the fallacy that MPs give a s*** about what 'ordinary people' think – they don't, they are in it for big fat pay-cheques and Whitehall dinners, don't pretend otherwise.

3 Kilroy is on around 9.30/10 in the morning – so who watches it or appears on it? I'll tell you who, Dole Spongers, liars leeching off disablilty, the unemployable,

gibbering old f******s, and students. And I'm sure you are aware about how much value and weight we give their opinions. Get a job, pay some tax and then maybe I might give a s*** what you have to say... but probably not.

And OAPs – just shut up already, if you haven't said everything you need to in seventy odd years, then you have wasted a lot of time repeating yourself.

4 Kilroy is a millionaire with a lavish lifestyle, he works five hours a week and ten minutes to do his shite newspaper column. So how does he qualify as an ordinary person?

Which brings me to another issue:

If we assume that Kilroy – which is on five times a week, for say forty-eight weeks a year for eighteen years – has as a guesstimate forty people in each audience. That's around 173,000 people who have appeared on Kilroy.

Has anyone ever met one? If so, did you ask them why they didn't take the chance to jam the smarmy tosser's microphone up his a***.

So, to extrapolate, if we take all audience participation shows, from *Family Fortunes* to *Question Time*, we are pretty soon going to run out of people in Britain to make up the audiences and contestants for this stuff.

So, of course, I have a theory:

I think there is a camp in the sticks where a crack team of 200 people are kept. They have all the disguises available to them and they rotate around the country making up audiences and panels. Every time you hear that vacuous cackling on the soundtrack to say Dinnerladies, or a particularly gormless looking Asian Doctor asks Robin Cook a question...

I'm telling you... It's one of the corp.

Anyway enough already, Kilroy, not just a patronising

s***bag, but a racist misinformed s***bag to boot.

Take him off the television for ever.

Oh and I see Richard Madeley of *Pinch & Judy* has come out in support of him as well, which is a further nail in the coffin. When that gibbering train wreck of an acquitted shoplifter crawls out of the woodwork it's a sure sign the wolves are circling. Do you know he went to the same school at John McVicar? I bet the jury didn't know that.

Congratulations Kilroy perhaps you can have discussions in the dole queue with a panel of the public on the subject of why 'I lost my job for being a useless f***wit'.

On British Royalty: 'Why Harry's Vices Are No Big Deal'
Western Daily Press

When it comes to being Royal, the Windsors, with very few notable exceptions, are just not very good at the job.

Imagine the position had been advertised, perhaps in the pages of *Country Life* or *The Tatler*:

'Wanted: One Royal Family to fill role in constitutional monarchy set-up. Must be good with horses and able to inspire loyalty and affection among subjects. Experience in wearing priceless jewels and in opening fetes and buildings an advantage. Handsome remuneration package includes extensive foreign travel, free gifts (which may be sold on) and grace and favour apartments for fringe relatives.'

If the current incumbents had applied, do you think they'd have got the job? Other than The Queen, would YOU employ any of them? Her Majesty is, on the whole, revered and respected, because she has such a clear sense of duty.

Sadly, most of her family often appear not to have the sense they were born with. They lurch from one public relations disaster to another, like a midnight choir of drunks tap-dancing on a tightrope. Failed marriages, allegations of homosexual rape, pilfering, selling each other down the river, there are few depths to which the Windsors will not sink, given the opportunity. This is chiefly because (a) They are not very bright and (b) They are badly advised.

It took the death of a princess to make the Windsors realise that they were wildly out of step with the huge majority of their subjects. Mind you, Diana was popular - which is not an adjective you ever see connected with Prince Edward, for one.

We are told that Edward, or the Earl of Wessex, to give him his ridiculous title, is the Queen's favourite child and in truth, he has a face that only a mother could love.

Worse, he has a disposition that only the saintly could forgive; I find it difficult to look at him without wondering how he would look handcuffed in a tumbril.

This selfish man wants it all, he demands the privacy and respect that he feels is his by birth, yet is not above milking his connections to make money.

He failed in the Royal Marines and he failed as an independent TV producer, and he would have done better to have named his company Abject productions, rather than Ardent.

The only thing ardent about Edward is his desire for wealth and privilege. Even his own brother can't stand him, but Charles, the brother in question, is another hard man to love, Camilla notwithstanding.

This is another selfish, sulky man who still travels the world with his own personal toilet seat. He retires in a huff whenever he fails to get his own way and throws plates and paddies when things are not exactly to his liking.

Like most of his family, he thinks that respect is his to command. Respect, even in Royal circles, has to be earned.

And how can anyone respect someone like Prince Andrew? What is he FOR exactly? Whenever we see pictures of him, he's sunning himself on some foreign jaunt, where he supposedly 'boosts' British business. How he does this has never been revealed, but being the son of the monarch clearly has something to do with it.

AS for his grim-faced sister, some will admire her for her charity work, but the rest of us will find it hard to forget or forgive her rudeness, barking at pensioners whose only 'crime' had been to queue up on a cold winter's morning to show their loyalty and devotion with a bunch of flowers.

And now we are told that the Queen is worried about Prince Harry and his propensity for a smoke. Well, Ma'am, there are more pressing matters that claim your attention. Harry is said to have been on the fags for years now, which concerns his granny, as well it might, since her late father's enthusiasm for the weed helped contribute to his early demise.

But if Harry's love of nicotine places him firmly in the ranks of the sinners, then we should remember that most folk would rather laugh with the sinners than cry with the saints. Other than his mother, who was the most popular Royal, ever? That's right, his great-granny, the Queen Mum, whose enthusiasms for drink, gambling and living beyond her means endeared her to the common people, even if she'd sooner have run the Derby on foot than spend any more time than she had to among the hoi-poloi.

The old Queen Mum understood that a job that required little more than a nice smile and a wave from time to time was a gig worth having. Being pleasant to people was just part of being at work.

No, the Queen would have much more to worry about if her grandson showed signs of sulkiness or a propensity for poncing around, instead of an understandable, human fondness for fags and a drink.

Wednesday is a special day, ma'am.

So don't worry. Instead, cry God for England, Harry and St George!

3

I've always said they should bring back Maggie

Burn More Witches, Say Tories
Summer of George: JustRamIt.co.uk

Social Security to be replaced with a food voucher system and 3 million bicycles attached to generators. All claimants will have to earn their meals by pedalling 5 hours a day to provide electricity. Pensioners to be harvested and ground up in huge vats to siphon off valuable nutrients and calciums that can be sold directly to the Middle Classes.

More single women to be investigated and subjected to the ducking stool then, if they are found to be a drain on the system or own a cat, to be set alight and burnt alive before they are drowned. Paedophiles, naturally, are to be castrated by use of a length of rope and a transit van.

Margaret Thatcher to be cryogenically frozen until such a time that she is needed to rise again and medical science has advanced enough to cure the side of her face and remove her senility. No tax whatsoever for anyone voting

Conservative. Farmers to be given exclusive rights to shoot any child above the age of criminal responsibility – 10 years old [Bulger case] – caught scrumping apples.

Statue of Kenny Everett not to be erected in Trafalgar square, even if Sam Taylor-Wood swears on affidavit that after he was dead she had regular unprotected anal sex with his corpse and is not HIV+.

RICHARD LITTLEJOHN on Cherie:
The Sun

The Wicked Witch is off on another of her cut-price holidays. She's taking Endora, Damien and the rest of the clan back to the palatial Government House in Bermuda.

We're told all travel and accommodation costs are being paid by the family. But local reports say she'll only have to pay $50 a night for her room – £27 at the current rate of exchange.

Where else in the world can you get that kind of value? You can't even get it in Bermuda. Government House is not available for rent to plebs. No doubt Tony will swing by on his way home from meeting Dubya in Washington, so they'll all get an upgrade on the way home.

I can't help thinking there are parallels between the WW and Posh Spice. Both are best known for their famous husbands these days. Both shamelessly exploit their children when it suits them. Endora is a permanent fixture, just like Posh's mum. Both their husbands have extra-marital, lovey-dovey relationships of which they disapprove – Becks with Rebecca Loos and Tone with Dubya.

And, just like Posh, the WW knows how to ruthlessly

exploit the Blair brand to get on in life and secure the best deal on everything from flats to schools, to holidays.

Difference is, the Beckhams pay their own way.

A POLITICAL PUNDIT on Michael Moore
Artnik

Michael Moore is a scumbag. Not because he's a completely unreliable, self-righteous, irresponsible, lying hypocrite, however. No, these are the things I can identify with. The reason Michael Moore is a scumbag is he caused one of the most shocking incidents in my life. I was reading a critique of Moore in the *Daily Mail*, which I agreed with word for word, when I glanced up at the byline and saw it had been written by Christopher Hitchens!

Hitchens is the most contemptible journalist on earth and I have never agreed with anything he's written nor will I ever again, but here is what he wrote about Moore: 'Europeans think Americans are fat, vulgar, greedy, stupid, ambitious and ignorant. And they've taken as their own, as their representative American, someone who actually embodies all those qualities.' Even someone as blinkered by hate as me can appreciate the truth when we see it, and Hitchens was right about Moore.

What makes Michael Moore so despicable is that every method that he criticises Bush for he employs in his own attacks on him. His defence to anyone who catches him out on some point is that 'desperate times call for desperate measures' and, yes,'the gloves are off', but he always insists that his documentaries paint a true picture in the

round. A recent defence of Moore noted that his critics' indictments are 'depressingly familiar': 'Moore's waistline invariably merits a snide mention, along with his luxurious Manhattan apartment, bullish manner and alleged manipulation of facts...' Excuse me, to say that a documentary maker is fat, rich and a high-liver is not in the same league as saying he manipulates the facts.

The accusation is even more onerous in Moore's case as he has a mission to save America, if not the world, from Bush. He also takes in a few other associated causes along the way, such as saving America from the NRA and Texas's death row inmates from the Bush family (baby-brother Jed took over from George the state governorship and is no less enthusiastic about the death penalty). These are heavyweight causes that demand exemplary standards of journalism. A documentary-maker who manipulates facts to make his points discredits his case and, with Moore, his claim to be taken seriously and not as some docu-comedian.

When accused of the same sorts of lies and inaccuracies as his political hate figures, Moore glibly sidesteps the issue by becoming plain ol' Mike the comedian. 'How can there be inaccuracy in comedy?' he winsomely shrugs. Well *Fahrenheit 9/11* is slightly different in import and tone from *Dr. Doolittle 2*! It is supposed to expose the truth of the Bush administration's record on terrorism (unless I really missed something...)

Moore left hypocrisy behind way, way back. He is a cynical, manipulative propogandist, which given his popularity is a lot uglier than he is himself. Of course, part of the reason he has gotten away with it is that a lot of the media with the clout to destroy him back off because, by and large, they think he is on the side of the angels. The only side Moore is on is his own fat bank balance and grotesque ego. Moreover, what he is doing to the integrity of political journalism is not dissimilar to putting a terrorist bomb under one of our democratic cornerstones. The Bush dynasty should be exposed but not by agitprops like Moore who can only expose the lies of others by lying themselves. In fact, by the way he does it, Moore displays a contempt for his audience which makes him less Bush's sworn adversary and more his kindred spirit.

JULIA ROBERTS on President Bush

He's embarrassing. He's not my president. He will never be my president. Republican comes in the dictionary just after reptile and just above repugnant... I looked up Democrat. It's of the people, by the people, for the people. He's for the rich, especially if they're from Texas.

[President George W. Bush made a state visit to the UK in Nov 2003. A number of public figures wrote him open letters]
Novelist Frederick Forsyth's letter to George Bush

Dear Mr President,
           Today you arrive in my country for the first state visit by an American president for many decades, and I bid you welcome.
   You will find yourself assailed on every hand by some pretty pretentious characters collectively known as the British left. They traditionally believe they have a monopoly on morality and that your recent actions

preclude you from the club. You opposed and destroyed the world's most blood-encrusted dictator. This is quite unforgivable.

I beg you to take no notice. The British left intermittently erupts like a pustule upon the buttock of a rather good country. Seventy years ago it opposed mobilisation against Adolf Hitler and worshipped the other genocide, Josef Stalin.

It has marched for Mao, Ho Chi Minh, Khrushchev, Brezhnev and Andropov. It has slobbered over Ceausescu and Mugabe. It has demonstrated against everything and everyone American for a century. Broadly speaking, it hates your country first, mine second.

Eleven years ago something dreadful happened. Maggie was ousted, Ronald retired, the Berlin wall fell and Gorby abolished communism. All the left's idols fell and its demons retired. For a decade there was nothing really to hate. But thank the Lord for his limitless mercy. Now they can applaud Saddam, Bin Laden, Kim Jong-Il... and hate a God-fearing Texan. So hallelujah and have a good time.

Salam Pax: The Baghdad Blogger

Dear George,

I hate to wake you up from that dream you are having, the one in which you are a superhero bringing democracy and freedom to underdeveloped, oppressed countries. But you really need to check things out in one of the countries you have recently bombed to freedom. Georgie, I am kind of worried that things are going a bit bad in Iraq and you don't seem to care that much. You might want it to appear as if things are going well and sign

71

Iraq off as a job well done, but I am afraid this is not the case.

Listen, habibi, it is not over yet. Let me explain this in simple terms. You have spilled a glass full of tomato juice on an already dirty carpet and now you have to clean up the whole room. Not all of the mess is your fault but you volunteered to clean it up. I bet if someone had explained it to you like that you would have been less hasty going on our Rambo-in-Baghdad trip.

To tell you the truth, I am glad that someone is doing the cleaning up, and thank you for getting rid of that scary guy with the hideous moustache that we had for president. But I have to say that the advertisements you were dropping from your B52s before the bombs fell promised a much more efficient and speedy service. We are a bit disappointed. So would you please, pretty please, with sugar on top, get your act together and stop telling people you have Iraq all figured out when you are giving us the trial-and-error approach?

Anyway, I hope this doesn't disturb you too much. Have a nice stay in London, wave hello to the demonstrators, and give my regards to your spin doctors. I bet they are having a hell of a job making you look good.

JULIE BURCHILL
'Writer'

George,
        Great job, keep it up!

[Artnik's attempts to ascertain whether Burchill was being ironic, sarcastic, rude or just simply enthusiastic disappeared into the black hole of her answerphone]

BEL LITTLEJOHN
Columnist

Dear President Bush,

I don't know if you know Janet Street Porter, but her motto is Tell it like it is. So let me tell you what it's like being me, right?

I've been away on sabbatical to research and write my new book, *Wotchoo Lookin' At...* and I arrive back in Blairland to find that for these past three years my son Marley has been lying on the green sofa in the basement in his Reeboks watching Eminem on MTV eating Big Macs, drinking Coke and surfing the internet for anything with Britney Spears on it.

What do all these have in common? Right first time, Georgie, baby. Country of origin: US of A.

What do you plan to do about it, then? Frankly, we in this country have been living under the American jackboot for far too long. As Harold Pinter so memorably put it in his recent poem:

> There's a bomb/Up your a***hole/Chum/And if you want to s**t it out/You can't/Chum/Because the president won't bloody let you/Chum.

The single human being I most admire in the world right now is Michael Moore. The guy's a genius. Talk about brave. If it wasn't for Moore, we'd never have discovered the link between Lee Harvey Oswald, the Osmonds, the tobacco multinationals, Pee-Wee Herman, Mark Chapman and Spiro Agnew. Nor would we now know that for four years in the 1980s Osama bin Laden was a fully paid-up member of the Disney Corporation, working first as a stoker on the Casey Jones Railroad Experience in

73

Disneyland Florida, and finally as a key member of the Three Bears in the Goldilocks House in Disneyland Paris. How to solve the whole Middle East thing? It would even be hard to solve just the Iraq problem in 200 words. But at least we can try. So first, George, let's for God's sake let bygones be bygones. I don't agree with your foreign policy, and – who knows? – maybe on reflection you don't agree with certain aspects of my forthcoming series of media studies seminars (Jade Goody and the Meaning of *Big Brother*) at the University of Oxbridge (formerly Thameside Polytechnic). But here's my advice – and it's advice I literally beg you, George, to take.

Take a few hours off. Light yourself a scented candle, dim the lights down low, and pick up Anita Roddick's wise and beautiful book, *Lessons I've Learnt from the Peppermint Shower Gel Tribe of East Africa*. Then read it, George – read it, and, believe me, you'll never want to go to war again.

BENJAMIN ZEPHANIAH
Poet

Bushwhacker,

Our prime minister was never very bright, and it is well known that he forgot his roots and developed an identity crisis, but that is no reason for you to take advantage of him. Before Tony met you he used to stay at home. OK, he would cause trouble sometimes and he could be rude to his people, but he didn't have plans to conquer the world. No, Bushy, before he met you, all he wanted to do was conquer the Tory party (and the Labour party) and play his guitar.

Stay away from him, you are leading him astray, you are corrupting his simple mind. He is now allowing his Muslim citizens to be tortured, and now he thinks we all look like your old friend Mr Bin Laden – the Rastas, the Sikhs, the hippies, in fact anyone who has travelled east in the last 30 years is nervous.

The thing is, Bushy boy, we don't trust you. We've seen what happens when you fall out with your friends, and we don't want to be bombed when you come looking for our weapons of mass destruction – and we have lots of them.

You say, 'In God You trust.' But God doesn't trust you... She told me.

[George and Laura Bush duly came over but he had other things on his mind than reading his letters]

Bush Visits UK, Declares American Independence
Watley Archives Review

President Bush finished a weeklong trip to the United Kingdom last Friday by officially announcing to Queen Elizabeth that America had declared independence.

'I have a little document here I think you ought to know about,' said Bush as he handed the surprised monarch a folded photocopy from his pocket during a ceremony at Buckingham Palace. 'It's called the Declaration of Independence.'

The president then faced the cameras and read forcefully from a card in his hand: 'When in the course of human events... well, whatever that means... what I mean is, that these united colonies (and that's us, now) are, and of right ought to be, free and independent states; that they are absolved from all allergies – allegation – allegiance to the British Crown. And that's you, ma'am.'

The unrehearsed event was evidently the president's own idea. 'Laura was telling me about the Declaration of Independence last week and I realised that no president had ever come over to give it directly to the king or queen of England. Can you imagine that? Now I can't explain why that is – I'm not an historian – but I'm a man of action, and I say it's time someone took care of this.'

Prime Minister Tony Blair, looking somewhat puzzled, emphasised in a press conference immediately afterwards that Bush's presentation of the Declaration would in no way impact the alliance between the US and the UK.

'Our joint resolution in the matter of Iraq is firm, and we do not foresee any changes in our resolve or our steadfast opposition to the forces instigating violence in the Middle East,' Blair assured reporters.

'Except for anything involving tea,' interrupted Bush. 'We had a little thing in Boston called the Boston Tea Party, and you might want to check that out before making unilateral tea-related decisions.' The president's announcement garnered mixed reactions from the world community.

'Well I am not really sure that this point needed a whole lot of clarification,' said UN Undersecretary-General of Economic and Social Affairs Jeffrey Goldberg. 'However, no one can dispute that George Bush was taking a stance on a very well-established cornerstone of American foreign policy which is probably beyond refutation.' Observers speculate that the president, beset by dwindling approval ratings and increasing opposition from the Democrats, was attempting to make a bold stance that would not be open to criticism.

The Queen offered no objection to the Declaration of Independence put forth by the president. 'Why would we object to the Americans leaving our commonwealth? For heaven's sake, we would be mad not to get rid of them' she said. 'Did you see what they did to the palace grounds?'

ALAN MASSIE on Modern Politicians
The Scotsman

Once upon a time politicians marked their authority by standing out from the crowd, although they might have a few populist tricks up their sleeves.

Things are different now. A politician must not only abide by the verdict of the democracy; he must show himself to be one of the boys – even if the boys are celebrities. So, for instance, Charles Kennedy seeks to win votes by appearing on that silly, and rather nasty, television programme, *Have I Got News For You* - the leader of a political party apparently believes that he will be taken more seriously by the electorate if he is seen to make a fool of himself.

Likewise, every politician is now expected to have a football team for which he professes a passionate attachment. One can't imagine Churchill or Macmillan sporting an Arsenal scarf, but both Tony Blair (Newcastle United) and Michael Howard (Liverpool) are keen to make their allegiance known.

William Hague was an exception, refusing to pretend to an interest he didn't share. What was the result? Hague lost his election and even the leadership of his party. He might have been wiser to have been seen cheering (or weeping) at Elland Road and assuring interviewers that the Tory Party came a poor second to Leeds United in his affections.

Thinking about these matters, it's tempting to indulge in a rant about the decadence of politics in our time, to go on about our debased democracy, mindless populism and all that. Yet politicians have always indulged in flattery for votes.

When learning is admired, politicians will show themselves to be erudite and quote Greek and Latin. When it isn't, they will happily appear on silly TV programmes and shout for their favourite football teams. Either way, they'll sock it to their chosen audience.

LONDON CABBIE on Tony Blair

Tony Blair? Don't make me laugh. *Phoney* Tony more like. If I see him and that hideous wife of his on the telly one more time I'll blow up the cab outside Number 10. Diabolical pair. If they want to go about the place playing king and queen that's fine by me but don't go pretending you're a 'Labour' leader. Don't you agree, guv?

Now, there's a couple of things he got right. Like Bombing the towelheads. Now I agree with him backing America on that. Trouble is we might all live to regret it. And like booting that Peter Mandelson out of the cabinet. I agree with that, but then he went and let him back in again. Now Pansy-Mandy's got a cushy number in Europe! Shirtlifters. Shut the front door on 'em and they're in by the back or the tradesman's entrance, more like it. I remember Mandy when he when he had one of those Cromwell Road moustaches. Shaved that off when Blair promoted him, didn't he?

And appointing that Ken Livingstone as Mayor was a good move. Livingstone's a diamond. If he's good to *newts* he's gotta be good *news*, I've always said. He's gawn and proved it, too, with the Congestion Charge. Okay, so not everyone likes it but that's politics ain't it? People say business is affected and whatnot, but for us cabbies it's worked a treat.

If you want my opinion, though, they should bring back Maggie. There's still life left in the old bird yet. She'd sort it all out. She sorted the Argies out didn't she? I tell yer she'd have the SAS onto that bin Laden in no time.

The man who would be king
Artnik

Since he came to power in 1997 Tony Blair ...
– halved the number of Prime Minister's question time in the House.
– spent little time in the commons apart from his one session of PMQ.
– said he put Britain at the heart of Europe, then postponed until he is re-elected having a referendum on the joining the euro.
– appointed more cronies to the lords than ANYONE else.
– made cabinet government all, and parliament nothing.
– went to war in Iraq on a false premise, then when every other leading politician in the world – including Bush – had accepted that Saddam's Weapons of Mass Destruction probably did not exist persisted in saying that he believed they would be found.
– said that he would do all in his power to sort out Africa's appalling military, political, economic and medical problems, then did nothing except send Foreign Secretary

79

and *ANOTHER* thing...

Jack Straw out on a photoshoot to Sudan while its militia were massacring more African farmers in six months than Saddam Hussein's regime killed in six years.
– used the media to make crucial announcements, thereby systematically cutting down the opportunity for debate.
– gave the green light to putting onto the statute book a bill that outlaws hunting foxes with dogs by agreeing to use the Parliament Act to prevent the Lords striking it out, then did not vote for it himself when it came before the House.
– professed to be a strong environmentalist, who supported the Kyoto Protocol on global warming, then refused to allow petrol prices to rise and refused to grasp the nettle of building more nuclear power plants.

QUENTIN LETTS on Alastair Campbell
the Daily Telegraph

Some 2,500 people almost filled Monday night's auditorium (despite the 'sold out' signs, there were, in fact, several empty rows at the back of the house). When Tony Blair's former press secretary loped on stage, there were some cheers and a few timid boos. Campbell's shoulders rolled with his pre-bout gait. His tongue gave a lizard-dart, in and out, and he cast a hooded eye at the throng, a buzzard scouring the valley floor for voles and fattish dormice.

What followed, however, was surprisingly ineloquent and dull. For the following 95 minutes, the almost mythically important Campbell, sometime 'real Deputy Prime Minister', once hailed as the cleverest communicator in Western politics, plodded and mumbled his way through a mixture of rant and anecdote.

His delivery was so poor that it was hard to hear many of his punchlines – and this from a man who upbraided ministers who failed to project their message with sufficient vigour.

As each minute passed, so faded the image of Campbell the Mighty, Campbell the Cruel. This New Labour mastermind, most cunning of Blair's Baldricks, turned out to be ... a bore.

Alastair Campbell is interesting only for what he has done. He is not interesting for the way he thinks, for his beliefs or philosophy. It makes him the most perfect embodiment, more perfect even than the Prime Minister himself, of that most unsatisfying, unintellectual thing, Blairism.

I hate your politics.
From Johnscalzi.com:

No, I don't know what they are. And no, I probably don't know who you are, either. Really, those two points are immaterial (no offence). As it turns out about, about 46% of you are liberal, 46% of you are conservative, and the rest of you just want your guns, drugs and brothels (here in the US, we call them folks 'libertarians').

Each of you carries baggage from your political affiliation, and all of that baggage has a punky smell to it, like one of your larger species of rodent crawled in and expired in your folded underwear. Listening to any of you yammer on about the geopolitical situation is enough to make one want to melt down one's dental fillings with a beeswax candle and then jam an ice pick into the freshly-exposed nerve, just to have something else to think about.

It's not so much that politics brings out the worst in people than it is that the worst in people goes looking for something to do, and that usually ends up being politics. It's either that or setting fires in trashcans.

In the spirit of fairness, and of completeness, let me go down the list and tell you what I hate about each major branch of political thinking.

Liberals: The stupidest and weakest members of the political triumvirate, they allowed conservatives to turn their name into a slur against them, exposing them as the political equivalent of the kid who lets the school bully pummel him with his own fists (Stop hitting yourself. Stop hitting yourself. Stop hitting yourself). Liberals champion the poor and the weak but do it in such condescendingly bureaucratic ways that the po' ill-educated plebs would rather eat their own shotguns than associate with the likes of them. Famously humourless and dour, probably because for a really good liberal, everything is political, and you just can't joke about things like that.

Defensive and peevish even when they're right. Under the impression that people in politics should play fair, which is probably why they get screwed as often as they do. Feel guilty about the freedoms their political positions allow them, which is frankly idiotic. Liberals are politically able to have all sorts of freaky mammal sex but typically don't; good liberal foreplay is a permission slip and three layers of impermeable barriers. The only vaguely liberal person we know of who seemed to enjoy sex in the last 30 years is Clinton, and look what he got out of it.

Fractious and have no sense of loyalty; will publicly tear out the intestines of those closest to them at the most politically inopportune times. The attention spans of poultry; easily distracted from large, useful goals by pointless minutiae. Not only can't see the forest for the trees, can't see the trees for the pine needles. Deserve every bad thing that happens to them because they just can't get their act together. Too bad those they presume to stand for get royally screwed as well.

Conservatives: Self-hating moral relativists, unless you can convince me that an intellectual class that publicly praises family values but privately engages in sodomy, coke and trophy wives is more aptly described in some other way. Not every conservative is an old wealthy white man on his third wife, but nearly every conservative aspires to be so, which is a real waste of money, youth, race and women. Genuinely fear and hate those who are not 'with' them -- the sort of people who would rather shit on a freshly-baked cherry pie than share it with someone not of their own tribe.

Conservatives believe in a government by the oligarchy, for the oligarchy, which is why the conservative idea of an excellent leader is Ronald Reagan, i.e., genial, brain-damaged and amenable to manipulation by his more mentally-composed underlings. Under the impression they own the copyright on Jesus and get testy when other political factions point out that technically Christ is in the public domain. Conservatives don't actually bother to spend time with people who are not conservative and, thus, become confused and irritable when people disagree with them; fundamentally can't see how that's even possible, which shows an almost charming intellectual naiveté. Less interested in explaining their point of view than nuking you

83

and everything you stand for into blackened cinders before your evil worldview catches on like a virus. Conservatives have no volume control on their hate and yet were shocked as Hell when Rush Limbaugh went deaf.

Conservatives clueless enough to think that having Condi Rice and Andrew Sullivan on the team somehow counts as diversity. Pen their 'thinkers' like veal in think tanks rather than let them interact with people who might oppose their views. Loathe women who are not willing to have their opinions as safely shellacked as their hair. Let their sons get caught with a dime bag and see how many are really for 'zero-tolerance'. Let a swarthy day labourer impregnate their daughters and find out how many of them are really pro-life.

Libertarians: Never got over the fact they weren't the illegitimate children of Robert Heinlein and Ayn Rand; currently punishing the rest of us for it. Unusually smug for a political philosophy that's never gotten anyone elected for anything above the local water board. All for legalised drugs and prostitution but probably wouldn't want their kids blowing strangers for crack; all for slashing taxes for nearly every social service but don't seem to understand why most people aren't at all keen to trade in even the minimal safety net the US provides for 55-gallon barrels of beans and rice, a crossbow and a first-aid kit in the basement. Blissfully clueless that Libertarianism is just great as long as it doesn't actually involve real live humans. Libertarians blog with a frequency that makes one wonder if they're actually employed somewhere or if they have loved ones that miss them.

Libertarian blogs even more snide than conservative

blogs, if that's possible. Socially slow – will assume other people actually want to talk about legalising hemp and the benefits of a polyamorous ethos when all these other folks really want is to drink beer and play Grand Theft Auto 3. Libertarianism the official political system of science fiction authors, which explains why science fiction is in such a rut these days. Libertarians often polyamorous (and hope you are too) but also somewhat out of shape, which takes a lot of the fun out of it.

Easily offended; Libertarians most likely to respond to this column. The author will attempt to engage subtle wit but will actually come across as a geeky whiner (Conservatives, more schooled in the art of poisonous replies, may actually achieve wit; liberals will reply that they don't find any of this humorous at all). Libertarians secretly worried that ultimately someone will figure out the whole of their political philosophy boils down to 'Get Off My Property'.

News flash: This is not really a big secret to the rest of us. I'm guessing you thought I was way off on your political philosophy but right on the button about the other two. Just think about that for a while.

Fed up with the new Big Brother
Internet rant

Have you ever asked yourself WHY you're are being tracked, categorised, filed, numbered, referenced, documented, classified, qualified, registered, indexed, recorded, listed and archived? Why any monetary transaction over a specified limit is traced by the Inland Revenue?

Why your cash withdrawals from your bank are tracked? Why anyone paying an airline ticket in cash is under suspicion? Why any person can now be searched and property seized without any charges?

Well, that's easy: 40+% of the workforce now get paid directly or indirectly by government. Never in history have so many been so successfully lied to and deceived by so many of their fellow citizens!

PETER HITCHENS on Immigration:
Mail on Sunday

The Government is deliberately hiding the truth about immigration. This is despicable in itself, and we are right to be angry about it. But anger by itself is useless.

The important thing is first to understand the scale of New Labour's project to change Britain into a multicultural nowhere land. Labour likes mass immigration for two reasons. One, it provides a constant excuse to censor the past and change the future. Two, it props up the economy which they have messed up with their enormous, uncontrollable welfare state. Welfare benefits at one end and penal taxation at the other mean that it simply isn't worth it for most British people to work for low-wage jobs.

But allow tens of thousands of illegal migrants into the country and you will then bring about an uncontrollable shadow economy, in which they slave away at essential tasks for misery wages which are only bearable-because they pay no taxes, working for bosses who wink at their illegal status.

This unscrupulous, cynical and destructive policy seems to me to be the real aim of New Labour. For reasons which baffle me, far too many voters cannot see this and are fooled by Labour's pretend policies cringingly promoted by feeble, tame newspapers and broadcasters.

CLARE ROWSON on hunting
Birmingham Post

How has it come about that a small handful of people are moulding a future for millions of others without any comprehension of what they are doing?

Hunting, and increasingly shooting and fishing, are being demonised by a small but vociferous number of Parliamentarians who have the strongest opinions dangerously matched by the weakest of knowledge. The politically correct crowd has declared open season on traditional country activities. The reasons for this vehement hostility are varied, but they all seem to boil down to one fact: those pursuing bans on hunting, on shooting and on fishing don't understand what it is they are against, nor do they care to learn. They are operating on moral autopilot, guided by class hatred and misdirected notions of animal welfare.

ANATOLE KALETSKY on Reigniting Class War
The Times

Anyone who believes that the ban on fox hunting is motivated by humanitarian principles or the generally sentimental attitude to animals in Britain today has totally failed to understand the political dynamics that have pushed this issue to the top of the Prime Minister's agenda.

There is no moral difference between a huntsman who find it exciting to chase a fox with dogs and a fisherman who finds it relaxing to torture a pike with a hook. In fact, opponents of hunting do not have a moral leg to stand on unless they campaign for a total ban on all other forms of unnecessary killing for pleasure, including the slaughter of animals for meat. The slaughter of animals is at least as 'cruel' and 'unnecessary' as the hunting of foxes... the only reason why cows are terrified and killed in abbatoirs is to provide us with a sensual pleasure – and a rather unhealthy one at that. Indeed, the only animal killing which is not essentially a human indulgence is medical research. Morally, vivisection is the only form of killing which can be fully justified.

Why, then, do opponents of hunting feel so passionately about saving foxes, but do not worry about the suffering of fish, cows and sheep. Why do so many of the same activists attack women wearing mink or sable, but do not give a damn about leather shoes? The difference is not about morality but about class and tribe. Hunting, like fur, is identified with the rich and the toffs. Fishing like leather and hamburgers is an indulgence of the urban working class.

HANS BLIX (UN Weapons Inspector)

It is somewhat puzzling, I think, that you can have a hundred percent certainty about the weapons of mass destruction's existence and zero percent certainty about where they are.

4

Seen Today's *Sun* Guv'nor?
Makes you fink

**ADAM HELLIKER after being fired from
the *Mail on Sunday* for 'improper conduct'**
Daily Telegraph

I'm only too aware that the *Mail on Sunday* is a publication
which has the highest morals and demands the utmost
probity in its endless endeavours to safeguard Middle
England from evil. I can only assume that their action in
stabbing one of their own in the back has been guided by a
righteous and higher power.
  [*Helliker's hanging offence was to privately and illicitly sell Lady Di's
  appointment diary to a collector, and back-pocket the £20,000 fee.*]

Western Daily Press:

I never cease to be amazed at what riles callers to my
phone-in programmes; regardless of the mayhem and
stupidity that surrounds us every day, just one mention of

the abuse of the English language and all hell breaks loose.

The trouble is, anyone on the radio who is foolhardy enough to launch into a debate on 'irritating phrases and superfluous words' is likely to get a severe drubbing from fanatical listeners who, you can guarantee, will have drawn up a list of 'language crimes' that you've regularly committed.

And so it was that my listeners ripped me apart for my alleged over-use of 'fantastic', 'extraordinary', 'absolutely' and 'there's more news at the top of the hour'. But it's hilarious to listen to the ranting peppered, as it is, with meaningless phrases.

I put forward a compelling argument for digging up the 'level playing field' and was even more convincing about the need to disbelieve that a village was 'trying to come to terms with' anything other than journalistic drivel.

As for 'plummeting down to earth' and a 'new innovation'; nothing plummets in any other direction than down and an innovation can hardly be old, can it?

But the real crackers are the absurd phrases that are used to give an appearance of intelligence, and yet, are totally meaningless. 'At this moment in time' is a stupid way of saying 'now', while 'by virtue of the fact' means 'because'.

So, to carry this to its extreme: 'I now find myself between a rock and a hard place as I, basically, address the issues surrounding singing from the same hymn sheet. Touching base with you, and hearing what you're saying could draw a line under it, but at the end of the day, it remains to be seen!'

WALTER HUMES on Cliches:
The Times

'...the most irritating phrases in the English language' has received plenty of media coverage. Of the top 10, I was particularly pleased to see the appearance of phrases that really mean the exact opposite of what they purport to say.

Thus, 'to be honest' often precedes a pack of lies. 'I hear what you're saying' signals a total disregard for your views. And 'with all due respect' might more truthfully be translated 'with utter contempt'. Other phrases which received a significant number of votes but did not quite reach the top 10 included 'the bottom line', 'between a rock and a hard place', 'it's not rocket science' and 'awesome'.

There were several contenders which are widely used in education circles such as 'prioritise', 'ongoing', 'value-added', 'singing from the same hymn sheet', 'moving the goalposts' and 'thinking outside the box'.

Whenever the term 'quality assurance' is used, the only thing that can be assured is that very little to do with real quality will feature.

The peddlers of the quality assurance gobbledygook are, of course, generally dull bureaucrats, a collection of bean counters who get pleasure from holding others accountable.

Another phrase that sets my teeth on edge is 'a culture of continuous improvement'. This is really a political slogan disguised as a professional principle. It is part of the 'feel good' rhetoric so beloved of politicians who prefer the soft sound bite to the hard thinking which is really needed.

91

In education, clichés are offensive because they are a lazy response to situations that call for serious thought. Next time you are confronted with one, try a little irony on the perpetrator. Say something like: 'Bear with me while I try to unpack your ideas. Tell me if I'm in the right ballpark.'

If I've got it wrong, no problem. By the way, some of your language is mind-boggling.'

MEDIA ANALYST on the British Press
Artnik

When the combined forces of the British press aren't bitching about celebrities, sportsmen or politicians, more often than not they'll be bitching about each other. *The Sun* vs. *The Mirror*, *The Mail* vs. *The Express* – frequently their front pages and leaders become no more than a tawdry, gloating catalogue of hatred for their (largely identical) rivals, full of scorn for their (largely identical) politics and condemnation of their (largely identical) professional malpractices.

The only losers in these playground battles are the readers – in whose name they are carried out, at whose expense they are conducted, and who for themselves are expected to believe that there are no more important news stories they should be hearing about. But it's not just the tabloids. *The Times* and *The Guardian* revel in the downfall of *The Telegraph*'s owner; *The Telegraph* bites back. All three of them get involved in price-fixing wars to try to drive *The Independent* back under. Every newspaper treats circulation figures as front-page news, and then presents them as they present all other news stories – that is, with unmerited sensationalism and great subjectivity.

And that is their right: its how the likes of Murdoch and Maxwell and Desmond and Black chose to spend their wealth. Of course, Black's undoing was to spend his shareholder's money, too. They bought newspapers so that they could own the truth. They care about money, sure – that partly explains their schemes to defame their rivals and steal their readers. But these modern philanthropists of Fleet Street, Wapping and the Wharf are not solely motivated by such base greed – largely, they are sickeningly rich already. No, what appeals to them is power: unelected, unanswerable, unmerciful power.

Most of them don't have what it takes to reach high political office, or perhaps already have too much of a chequered past. The public wouldn't like them, there are too many hoops to jump through – besides, they don't want *their* name dragged through the mud in the public eye. Most of all there is too much responsibility when you are an 'elected' official: social responsibility, ethical responsibility.

You deal in security not profit. The money you wield is not yours, it is the taxpayers' – and it is to their votes your position is accountable, not those of your friends on the board. So why not run a newspaper instead? You have the Prime Minister's ear. You have the power to play kingmaker and influence policy. And you can tell millions of people what to think while pretending you are representing their views.

So no wonder they turn on rival groups and rival editors when they find that they are not operating in a monopoly. But what is more interesting is when they work together.

93

There is only one time you'll find *The Sun* standing up for the Mirror, or *The Guardian* enjoying the support of *The Telegraph*. That is when the integrity of **news itself** is under threat. Oh, and by 'news' I don't mean facts and events. They will always persist. I mean the **news industry**: the right to use and abuse news as you choose. So look at the editorials next time a court rules that a newspaper broke the law to sell a story. See whose side *The Sun* takes if Naomi Campbell sues *The Mirror* for invasion of privacy.

When these relatively uninteresting rulings are taking place in our free and independent courts – things that shouldn't really affect the life of the ordinary citizen, stuff like how long range a lens you can use to film a newlywed naked, and whether or not it's legal to assist in a crime in order to sell the story – just have a read of the opinion columns across the board. From the mighty Thunderer's leading article, to the cheeky Nikkala, 23, from Norwich, as she parrots out the party line in her News in Briefs column. They will all chime with one accord: 'The freedom of the press is the SINGLE MOST IMPORTANT ISSUE IN BRITAIN TODAY.'

Don't believe a word of it. It is, quite probably, the LEAST pressing issue of our time. This is not Communist Russia or Fascist Spain, whatever parliamentary sketch wags tell you about this Labour government. People can speak their minds. We have an opposition. And we have a free press. TOO f****** free. They get away with murder, with propaganda, with defamation and lies. They consider it their duty to mess with people's careers and judge their private lives (whereas journalists never take coke, never get involved in bad business and NEVER sleep with their secretaries). They hideously appropriate horrific events like the death of a princess or the murder of a child to their own grotty campaigns designed to boost circulation. They lump all society's ills on one-off paedophile bogeymen while peddling cheap sex, lascivious coverage of rape cases and sexual images of under-age girls. If there is a sex-monster epidemic in this land, then we all know who contributed to the problem. They run count-downs to 16-year-old model's birthdays so they can show us their tits. They award Charlotte Church the Rear of the Year retrospectively for a year in which she was under-age. They tell people about 'sick websites' and 'sick paedo manuals' which then get more hits and more sales then ever before. And they WILL NOT accept responsibility. Not responsibility for other people's crimes – but the one they have to the greater social good. A responsibility which they daily abuse for both money and self-promotion.

I f****** hate them all.

MALCOLM RIFKIND on British newspapers
Artnik

I have a deep dislike, nay loathing, for the way in which our newspapers, and not just the tabloids, mangle the English language and treat their readers as good for bread and circuses and little else.

There was a time when you could assume that the main story on the front page really was the most important event since the last edition. Now the tabloids compete with one another for titillation while the so-called quality press are little better.

The Times will report some uninteresting interview it, alone, has had as the story of the day in order that it can trumpet it as an 'exclusive' . *The Independent* has ceased putting news on its front page preferring some photograph and text of the 'J'accuse' variety.

And all of them go in for unashamed exaggeration. If some thoughtful judge decides not to imprison some miscreant the relatives of the victim are, invariably, described as 'outraged' or 'disgusted' which is, as often as not , the term that the journalist has offered them rather than the reaction they have volunteered.

Minor peccadilloes of ministers , clergymen or judges are invariably 'scandals' while harmless members of the Royal Family are lampooned and traduced. Such turgid journalism is justified, and not just by the Piers Morgans, as 'in the public interest'. It rarely is. There is a great difference between the 'public interest' and 'the public are interested' but it is a distinction our newspapers do not recognise.

Of course, they always get the last word. Some years ago a local paper reported that 'Half the councillors are corrupt'. When there were great protests and demands for an apology the editor reluctantly agreed. He printed his retraction under the headline 'Half the councillors are not corrupt'.

JONATHAN SWIFT on Critics

I must be so bold, to tell my criticks and witlings, that they are no more judges of me, than a man who is born blind can have any true idea of colours. I have always observed that your empty vessels sound loudest: I value their lashes as little as the sea did when Xerxes whipped it. The utmost favour a man can expect from them, is that which Polyphemus promised Ulysses, that he would devour him the last: They think to subdue a writer as Caesar did his enemy, with a Veni, vidi, vici. I confess, I value the opinion of the judicious few, but for the rest, to give my judgment at once, I think the long dispute among the philosophers about a vacuum, may be determined in the affirmative, that it is to be found in a critick's head. They are, at best, but the drones of the learned world, who devour the honey, and will not work themselves; and a writer need no more regard them, than the moon does the barking of a little senseless cur. For, in spite of their terrible roaring, you may with half an eye discover the ass under the lion's skin.

KURT COBAIN on *Rolling Stone*

At this point in our career, before hair-loss treatment and bad credit, I've decided that I have no desire to do an interview with *Rolling Stone*. We couldn't benefit from it because the average *Rolling Stone* reader is a middle-aged ex-hippie-turned-hippiecrite who embraces the past as 'the glory days' and has a kinder, gentler, more adult approach towards liberal conservatism. The average *Rolling Stone* reader has always denied underworld musical options unless they become an obviously safe commodity.

I've always felt it was necessary to help out the 'Now Generation' internally destroy the enemy by posing as or using the enemy. But the 'Now Generation' doesn't read *Rolling Stone*. So we'll just sit around and wait until the old school starves like dinosaurs while the diaper school begins to litter the floors of Wall Street with 'Real Love'

97

revolutionary debris. Smells like thirtysomething.

I would only wear a tie-dyed shirt if it were dyed with the urine of Phil Collins and the blood of Gerry Garcia. Hope I die before I turn into Pete Townshend.

'DAVE' on the *Evening Standard Magazine*
Internet

If you're anything like me and actively enjoy putting yourself through cultural purgatory at least once a week, then you're probably an avid reader of the *Evening Standard*'s *ES* magazine, too. It really is very, very bad indeed: written for people called Hugo, Toby, Marianne and Belinda, by people called...er...Hugo, Toby, Marianne and Belinda; grotesquely self-satisfied and smug; galaxies away from the lives lived by the vast majority of Londoners.

You can just imagine the world inhabited by the people responsible for this publication. Folks who actually know and care who Nicky Haslam is but reckon the unemployed are a mass of workshy parasites who should be made to do something for their money (recognise the irony?), financially stable, well educated, well spoken and, most importantly, well protected from the hardships of modern existence; cosseted, privileged and, in their minds, absolutely entitled.

In fact, reading through this rag often makes me think of this passage from Tom Wolfe's *Bonfire Of The Vanities*: 'It was a ten-dollar ride each morning, but what was that to a Master of the Universe? Sherman's father had always taken the subway to Wall Street, even when he was the chief executive officer of Dunning Sponget & Leach... But

to the r
Sherma
That wa
used. 'I
Sherma
meaning

That's rig

Compelli
more than
see and
inverted s
these peop
this week i
a feature h

and ANOTHER thing...

down roots. But thanks to likes of
'creative', media professional' pals
loosely fit this description, too), th
the area. Not living a hand-
benefits and social disenfra
her house, a Cartier
'expensive private ed
for two pages of
neighbours mak

That, to
eat, havi
stake i
con

The s   brought up in an
Elizabethan manor house in Norfolk, Sophie Leris now
finds herself lulled to sleep by the sound of gunfire in
Hackney. And she's not alone, she says—we've seen
Nouveaux Pauvres, but never this pauvre...'

Now I'm sorry, like Ms Leris, I lived at the end of the
38 bus route for two years, probably just down the road
from her, and not once did I find myself dozing off to the
sound of Glocks being discharged, nor did I ever feel at any
discernible risk of anyone busting a cap in my proverbial.

While I'm fiercely proud of my 'hood and love it like
I've never loved anywhere I've lived, it's true that life can
be tough there. The crack heads, nutballs, hookers and
muggers are very real, but they're not what I'm talking
about. Generations of families live in Hackney, people
work and bring up kids there; it's an okay place to put

ur Soph and her
(and, yes, I know I
ey're being priced out of
o-mouth existence of state
nchisement, this woman owns
watch, talks of her children's
cations' and probably earned more
atrocious writing than many of her
e in a fortnight.
me, is not poor. Poverty is not being able to
g no educational/career prospects, no voice or
n society. As long as people still live under these
ditions, it's not a term we should throw around lightly.
could quote from this piece ad nauseam, example after
example of whinnying self-pity and breathtaking
insensitivity, but I won't. It's simply too ghastly.

MARK THOMAS on Lads' Mags
New Statesman

It was a brief and charmless flirtation, and now, after two
editions, my career as a columnist for the new lads'
magazine *Zoo Weekly* has come to an end. In case you
hadn't noticed, a bunch of weekly lads' mags has been
launched this year. They feature a high celebrity nipple
count, football stuff, endless top ten lists, and a good dollop
of graphic injury/snuff photos. In between is woven the odd
article and column.

When Ben Knowles, a nice man and an ex-editor of the
New Musical Express, asked if I would write for *Zoo*, I
wanted to know what they expected me to write about.

Reassured that the normal mix of a couple of gags, an extended rant and a dash of utter hatred for politicians would be fine, I wanted to know a bit more about the publication.

It's a basic lads' mag, except weekly,' said Ben. A prominent picture in the mag shows a woman mastur-bating, with a cat's head where her vagina should be, accompanied by a quip about the size of pubic lice these days. This is the kind of website trash that bored office workers email to each other to break the monotony of the day.

A list of top ten terrorist organisations is merely an excuse to show a photo of soldiers parading over body bags. Two items appear about a survey that shows women like sex with strangers.

It is predictable, voyeuristic and dull. Its pseudo-prole culture of the uberdog begs for it to be read by City boys. 'Look at a picture of these w***ers,' it cries. 'Everyone is a tosser but you! Everything is a commodity. Everything exists for your pleasure.'

I read one edition and stopped writing my column. Obviously, this was an error of my own making, and I should have known better. So I have ordered an inquiry into my behaviour. Fortunately, I have been completely exonerated.

MEDIA ANALYST on Piers Morgan
Artnik

Even Piers Morgan's face is unpleasant. He looks as if he's permanently trying to hide the fact that he's a little bit out of breath. He resembles nothing so much as a prep school games master desperately hoping the boys don't notice that they've worn him out. It's not his lack of physical appeal

which makes him so obnoxious, though. It's his arrogance. He rebranded *The Mirror* in the wake of 9/11 as a 'serious' tabloid, as if the move was somehow a tribute to the murdered New Yorkers. It was, in fact, an obvious and commercially vital move to capture a niche in the tabloid market. It would be no good to be saying the same things as *The Sun*. Honest, crusading Piers hated *The Sun*.

Except he used to love it. Just don't expect him to admit it in his 'eagerly awaited' autobiography. In 1991 he paid tribute to then editor Kelvin Mackenzie in the most fulsome terms: 'He actually comes to me and says, Shouldn't we do something on Vanilla Ice? How many tabloid editors would even think of that? That's why he's such a good editor...' He went on to brag that 'I've never paid out a penny in a libel action. A lot of people have tried, but a lot of people have backed down. I'm not saying that makes me a paragon of virtue but that is a fact. Nobody has proved in court that I have made up a story...'

Again, don't expect to read it in the autobiography. Thirteen years ago our Piers was so virtuous that he was able to say that if people thought he would ever make something up '...they're living under a massive misapprehension...'

Perhaps it was this unimpeachable purity that prompted him to boast that 'I get paid as much as the Prime Minister...But it's all relative, you know...I work very hard...' Why was Piers worth such a salary, you might ask. Well, because '...I get on with Phil Collins, I get on with David Bowie, I get on with Jason Donovan, I get on with Kylie Minogue...That's my job, to build myself up as a friend of the stars and make it all very chummy...'

Tragically, the stars were not evident in force when

Piers was sacked as editor of *The Mirror* earlier this year for printing fake photographs of military brutality in Iraq. Perhaps we should have realised it would end like this when he admitted all those years ago that 'I'm not averse to nice stories, but I prefer nasty stories...' Only difference being that in 1991, Piers was still just about honest enough to slip in the afterthought 'If they're true...'

JON KELLY AND DAVID EDWARDS on Americanisms
Daily Mirror

We must stop using these ghastly American expressions. Do yourself a favour and speak proper English. Here are some of the worst culprits:

Closure – There was a time when this was what happened after last orders at the Crown and Ferret. Now we're talking the pop psychology of Oprah Winfrey.

'Closure' may be more succinct than: 'I have finally reconciled myself to my parents' divorce, which for years impeded my psychological development', but who needs it when the old English way - lifelong bitterness - was so much more satisfying?

Issues – Once teenagers had spots and dodgy hairstyles; today they have 'issues'. Favourites include minor parental neglect, being denied the latest pair of trainers and the way Mum is so embarrassing in front of friends.

Next time you hear some Avril Lavigne-alike airing her 'issues' at the mall (or Tesco's car park), just stop her and say: 'Real issues are Iraq or the environment. You haven't got issues, you've got acne.'

Apartment – It's the same size as a flat, it looks like a

flat, yet by calling it an apartment, estate agents can charge you an extra £80,000. All you get extra is the misguided belief that people called Ross and Rachel will drop by for brunch.

Face it: you're renting a one-bed flat over the chippie, and nobody's coming round except for the rent.

Can I get...? – When Jennifer Aniston says it in Friends, she really means: 'May I have...' An example of the States' grab-and-go coffee-bar culture which sounds outrageously silly over here. The correct response from cafe staff to the question: 'Can I get a coffee?' should, of course, be: 'No you can't get it. You see, I work here, so that's   my   job.'

Retail outlets – Remember when these used to be called 'shops'? Outlets are surely best left in the remit of sewage firms. As are some shops.

New World-style – Stock expression used whenever a European wine producer makes something that tastes ripe or has a bold label. Conversely, whenever a New World producer makes something that doesn't taste of strawberry jam, it will be described as 'straddling the gap between the New and Old World'

Bringing the pub experience into the home – Some brewers can genuinely replicate the blandness of their nitrogenated ales in a canned format. But they cannot guarantee overflowing urinals, stroppy bar staff and a slobbering St Bernard that keeps pestering you for peanuts.

The customer is king – This is almost certainly not true, though if Juan Carlos does occasionally nip into your shop for a few bottles of Don Darius and a packet of Pringles, we stand corrected. It is possible that you would like to publicly guillotine the awkward sod who barracks you for not stocking Mackesons and then, when you do finally get some in, is never seen again but that doesn't make him a king.

When it's gone, it's gone – You don't say! We thought that there was really a never-ending supply of £2.49 Rioja from that producer we'd never heard of. Next you'll be telling us that the story of the Magic Porridge Pot was made up.

Brewed from the finest ingredients – You name it the choicest hops, the finest barley, the purest water and a bespoke strain of yeast that has to be kept in an armour-plated fridge and guarded by wolves. Yes, there's no doubt about it with such Grade A ingredients, this is the best beer money could possibly buy. Weird how the brewery has just announced it's being axed.

Or simply on its own – The inevitable punch line that follows a long list of recommended food pairings on a wine's back label. This presumably allays any confusion in the mind of the poor consumers, lest they think it is compulsory to enjoy the wine with chicken jalfrezi, Bolivian-style gravadlax, or roast ox and neeps in a loganberry jus.

Best served chilled – A default piece of advice on the labels of white wines and lagers. Frequently doubles up as a public service announcement, since you need to chill some of these products to within an inch of their lives in order to avoid tasting them.'

5

Now, don't get me wrong,
I'm not one of those there racialists, BUT...

A XENOPHOBE on The Swiss
Artnik

Not too many people seem to have a problem with the Swiss. Neutral, you see. Liberal. Peace-loving.

And with all those wonderful winter sports and buxom milkmaids to be getting on with, who can blame them for not wanting to get mixed up in something as trivial as the defence of the free world? 'Don't look at us,' they said.

'We didn't start it. We'll stay at home skiing, yodelling and helping keep both sides stocked up with vital supplies of novelty clocks.

But we will take your money. Oh yes. Even after the war's over and the winner has been declared, the villains' money is still good round these parts. We'll take your gold and clean off the blood. That's not the same as actually *doing* it, is it? And in years to come every fugitive, fraudster, tax dodger, terrorist and aristocrat can use our banks to hide their wealth from prying eyes. They'll even get a free watch. We won't ask any tough questions, especially not of ourselves, as we cream healthy chunks off the top to fuel our own insatiable appetite for rich chocolate.'

Well I for one won't stand by and take their hypocrisy a moment longer. They're not so damn neutral when we beat them at football then ask them to send an honest referee to adjudge our game against Portugal. So if you ask me their moral logic is like their cheese – *a load of old s**t*.

Another race linking cheese and cowardice would be the French. Their crimes against humanity are too obvious, too universally recognised to waste my time on here. But that's not going to stop me. Whether it's giving up Paris to the Nazis in less time than it took to say, 'Mais oui Monsieur Hitler,' or failing to back President Bush in a justified and popular war on Iraq (a decision which is now making them look pretty stupid), the French would rather live on their knees than stand up and fight. Come to think of it a Frenchman is never happier than on his knees, most likely with his trousers down, trying to use one of their disgusting lavatories that don't have seats.

In fact the only time the French ever knuckle down and show a bit of fight is when they're up against defenceless animals. Horses, for example. Or geese, which they force-feed butter through tubes after clamping their beaks, just so they can gorge themselves on the goo when the poor animal's liver finally explodes. I'm not saying the results aren't delicious – just that I would only buy Foie Gras from an ENGLISH supermarket.

Or consider the delicate and placid Ortolan, a beautiful and rare songbird which passes over France but once a year. The reasons for this become obvious when you realise

Now, don't get me wrong, I'm not one of those there racialists, BUT...

that it is a national pastime over there to capture the bird, blindfold it, then lock it in a box with nothing but piles of honeyed figs. When the poor creature has binged to four times its normal size, it is paralysed with a single shot of armagnac straight to the heart, then drowned alive in a tub of hot brandy. The victim is presented to the richest, fattest man in the region, who cools the corpse by popping it whole into his salivating jowls and cracking its bones at the neck, then slowly pulling the pretty head from between his front teeth by the beak. All this he performs while hiding his face under a cloth in a mixture of pride and shame.

It is a measure of the man – and an indictment of his people – that for his last meal national hero President Mitterand ordered 30 of these endangered canaries, these living truffles, and stuffed himself to death. No doubt his friends and families then feasted on his still-beating liver and what remained of his heart.

And yet THEY tell us we can't even eat bendy cucumbers, or deep-fry pork pies.

Speaking of battered junk food, what about the Scottish? They're no better, with their ginger hair and even more ginger approach to opening their wallets. Their entire national identity is predicated on the hatred of a neighbouring nation which has actually done something with its life, like conquer the world. The only thing the Scots have ever conquered are the Hebrides. What good are they to anyone? They're welcome to their independence, along with the Welsh, and in return they can stop cropping up in our parliament every week to demand subsidies. The same goes for the Irish, like all Celts so eaten up by an inferiority complex they simply turn to drink. Which brings us back to the Scots.

The truly sad thing is their assumption that the English hate them in return. In fact most English people don't even know where Scotland *is*, only occasionally hearing about it when we're drawn against them in some World Cup group alongside Greece and Moldova.

God, *Moldovans*, don't even get me started on them. But as for Greece, that's a sorry state of affairs. They can win a game of football but they can't even build a stadium in time for kick-off. They had over 2000 years to prepare for hosting the Olympics again but by the time it started they had only successfully completed a brothel, some novelty amphora and one javelin - but even that was a bit warped off to one side. They seem to think just because they invented poetry and modern thought that gives them the right to lord it over us. *Well don't forget what else they invented – and you don't see them shouting about THAT from the rooftops, now do you?*

God, all these Spanish and Italian girls prefer it 'in the Greek fashion' because of bloody Catholicism. Well they may get to heaven but they won't have much fun spending eternity with a collapsed rectum.

Which brings me neatly back to the French.

They've produced nothing in the way of art or music. They have no justifiable basis for their pretension or cultural snobbery. They trumpet a cinematic tradition which churns out glorified pornography, and condemn Hollywood as the devil, whereas in fact the most successful film in French box-office history is Jurassic Park. That's because all their own filmmakers can produce are puerile comedies about time-travelling midgets or joyless urban romances which all end with the husband, wife, mistress and lesbian best friend getting together to discuss their sex lives in a café off the Place Monmartre. I HATE French cinema.

But not as much as Swedish cinema. No wonder they're all killing themselves, good Christ it's depressing. But there's not much to do once you switch off the telly. However early you start watching it'll always be dark by the time the film's over, and then you've got no option but to listen to *Dancing Queen* one last time and blow your head off.

The only thing the Swedes can boast that's more boring than their films is their football team. In turn the only thing more boring than the Swedish football team is the Norwegian one. God, it's a wonder they're not throwing themselves into the fjords as well. But at least they're better than the Dutch. Those lazy pot-smoking weasels, piling over here in droves for their stag weekends to drink our strong lager and enjoy two hedonistic days free of narcosis and strip bars. Are they intent on building a new Sodom and Gomorrah founded on drugs and hookers, as if continental Europe wasn't already fit to burst with loose women and people talking senseless gobbledygook?

And no-one speaks more rubbish than the French. Which makes it even stranger they should have a dedicated government institute for preserving that ugly braying noise that streams from their mouths with all the elegance and self-control of a Parisian gourmand dribbling at a chorus line of fat-legged frogs in tutus doing the can-can.

L'Academie Francaise, as they call it, is one of the most

sinister and egregious institutions in the world, comparable with Al'Qaeda and the Vatican. It's sole purpose is to promote the use of the French language and to prevent it evolving to meet the demands of the modern world, to which unfathomable end the government have afforded it more power than the police force. They make it their business to fine broadcasters, advertisers and writers for daring to branch out into English or American English – whereas in those countries it may be considered quite dashing to slip in the odd bit of French. Once caught, these wretched 'thought-criminals' pay the price of their education – suffering fines, jail or worse, and their families never hear from them again.

That's the kind of heavy-handed tyranny we'd expect from a South American military despot – but let's not forget that every corrupt South American is essentially a Spaniard at heart. It must make the real Spaniards and Portuguese sick to their bellies to see their distant cousins lording it up in cocaine-fuelled dictatorships while they're left nurturing cork and olives in third-world conditions relying on hand-outs from the EU.

In fact, these countries are the poor cousins of Europe AND the rest of the world. As their Latin counterparts revel in stunning beaches, for their holidays the European progenitors must hack their way through thick smoke and greasy chip paper in English colonies like Torremolinos. The Brazilians and Puerto Ricans have some of the most beautiful woman in the world; the average Iberian can't even afford his stumpy wife's electrolysis bill.

Which is not to say Eastern European women are any more desirable for being six-foot-tall, bony and blonde. Whenever you meet a stunning Russian or Czech, look to

113

her mother. After a certain age – normally early in their thirties – ALL Balkan beauties suddenly transform into a rumpled midget called Olga, their faces alive with moles sprouting thick black hair. There are no exceptions to this rule.

Which rigid rule of law brings us finally to the Germans. Well actually I LIKE the Germans.

They had a few ideas that they got right and a few they got wrong. But at least they had the guts to put their hands up and admit they lost – or at least, one hand. They are efficient and organised and no-nonsense. The fact is, as I have conclusively demonstrated, there are many arguments for bringing the old jackboot down on most of mainland Europe. Empire-building is an admirable concept, done properly, often the only effective way to force your ideas down other people's throats (the French method only works on poultry). Putting aside the one or two crackpot theories of a lone madman (along with his generals and cabinet ministers and footsoldiers, of course), the German people have everything to be proud of in their contributions to modern Europe. It's not like they voted him in or anything. In fact when German TV ran a parallel show to our own Great Britons, they actively refused to count any of the millions of votes cast for Adolf Hitler.

The only mistake was of the German imperial plan was not dispensing with Europe as a bad show altogether – and picking instead on far-flung countries to with poorer resources, weapons and medicine. This is what made Britain great - and by Great Britain, I do of course mean England.

Which reminds me, about those French...

JOHNNY DEPP on America

America is dumb, it's like a dumb puppy that has big teeth that can bite and hurt you, aggressive. My daughter is four, my boy is one. I'd like them to see America as a toy, a broken toy. Investigate it a little, check it out, get this feeling and then get out.

I was ecstatic they re-named 'French Fries' as 'Freedom Fries'. Grown men and women in positions of power in the U.S. government showing themselves as idiots.

TOBIAS SMOLLETT on the French
Travels through France and Italy (1766)

If a Frenchman is admitted into your family, and distinguished by repeated marks of your friendship and regard, the first return he makes for your civilities is to make love to your wife, if she is handsome; if not, to your sister, or daughter, or niece. If he suffers a repulse from your wife, or attempts in vain to debauch your sister, or your daughter, or your niece, he will, rather than not play the traitor with his gallantry, make his addresses to your grandmother; and ten to one, but in one shape or another, he will find means to ruin the peace of a family, in which he has been so kindly entertained. What he cannot accomplish by dint of compliment, and personal attendance, he will endeavour to effect, by reinforcing these with billet-douxs, songs, and verses, of which he always makes a provision for such purposes. If he is detected in these efforts of treachery, and reproached with his ingratitude, he impudently declares that what he had done was no more than simple gallantry, considered in France as an indispensable duty on every man who pretended to good breeding. Nay, he will even affirm, that his endeavours to corrupt your wife, or deflower your daughter, were the most genuine proofs he could give of his particular regard for your family.

If a Frenchman is capable of real friendship, it must certainly be the most disagreeable present he can possibly make to a man of a true English character. Your French friend intrudes upon you at all hours: he stuns you with his loquacity: he teases you with impertinent questions about your domestic and private affairs: he attempts to meddle in all your concerns; and forces his advice upon you with the most unwearied importunity: he asks the price of every thing you wear, and, so sure as you tell him, undervalues it, without hesitation: he affirms it is in a bad taste, ill-contrived, ill-made; that you have been imposed upon both with respect to the fashion and the price; that the marquise of this, or the countess of that, has one that is perfectly elegant, quite in the bon ton, and yet it cost little more than you gave for a thing that nobody would wear.

If there were five hundred dishes at table, a Frenchman will eat all of them, and then complain he has no appetite. This I have several times remarked. A friend of mine gained a considerable wager on an experiment of this kind: the petit maitre ate of fourteen different plates, besides the dessert; then disparaged the cook, declaring he was no better than a marmiton, or turnspit.

A French friend tires out your patience with long visits; and, far from taking the most palpable hints to withdraw, when he perceives you are uneasy, he observes you are low-spirited, and therefore declares he will keep you company. This perseverance shows that he must either be void of all

116

penetration, or that his disposition must be truly diabolical. Rather than be tormented with such a fiend, a man had better turn him out of doors, even though at the hazard of being run through the body.

Vanity predominates among all ranks, to such a degree that they are the greatest egotists in the world; and the most insignificant individual talks in company with the same conceit and arrogance, as a person of the greatest importance. Neither conscious poverty nor disgrace will restrain him in the least either from assuming his full share in the conversation, or making his addresses to the finest lady, whom he has the smallest opportunity to approach: nor is he restrained by any other consideration whatsoever. It is all one to him whether he has a wife of his own, or the lady a husband; whether she is designed for the cloister, or pre-engaged to his best friend or benefactor. He takes it for granted that his addresses cannot but be acceptable; and, if he meets with a repulse, he condemns her taste, but never doubts his own qualifications.

I hope your entire race gets mad cow disease
www.scankybitch.nz

I am sick of politically correct. *'You must think like us or else.'* Bulls**t. Racism is wrong. OK I agree, at no point in your life should you EVER say, 'What's he doing here, he's a nigger.' You should never dislike someone or not want to talk to someone based on the colour of their skin but for f*** sake people lets not take it to the 'I was going to slap my wife but ended up carving her head off, breaking every finger and crucifying her upside down on the garage door' extreme.

I am a middle class, white New Zealander with European descendants... I can't f****g say anything about anybody. I am not allowed to say the word 'Nigger' to black men and even calling a man Black is borderline abuse. I cannot these days even talk about race differences or culture differences without people looking at me sideways wondering if I belong to the KKK in my spare time.

I mean, THE F**K?? I don't have enough time in my day to sleep, eat, piss, game, sleep and work without cutting up my goddam bed sheets (who the hell has white bed sheets anyway, sure it's the same colour as those embarrassing stains but chocolate, blueberries and caramel look so much worse), run around the rural landscape burning the Afro-America inhabitants of New Zealand.

I want my speech back. I love to talk about cultures, differences and why we are not all the same. Face it, people, we are not the same. Each race has its quirks and, if we cannot talk about them in the open, how the hell are we ever going to understand each other. I have had enough, I would rather be living under a bridge, snorting glue than not be able to poke at other cultures in a derogatory manner for a second longer.

Asians:
Asians are accused again and again of bad driving. I have to say as a group, their driving ability is fairly bloody average. However, I think it is not the skill that is the issue, it's the fact they act like no one else is using the road. I have lost count of the number of times I have been caught behind an Asian driver who decides they are looking for something and drive down a busy street, hugging the centre line at ONE KILOMETRE AN HOUR. They do the same

things on side walks, forming big groups of people and standing right in the middle of the sidewalk: I AM HERE and if you don't like me doing what I am doing SCREAM AND YELL AND HONK AT ME because believe you me, pal, I have a full blown arsenal of VACANT, CONFUSED looks I am more than ready to throw out at you.

Islanders:
Men should not wear skirts with flowers on them.

French:
I hope your entire race gets mad cow disease, foams at the mouth and then slowly melts into puddles of filth that smells and looks exactly like Tomato sauce. You are all arrogant bastards and you have done enough to New Zealand to warrant us sending a three man squad to force your entire army into submission.
While you are at it you owe me and every other New Zealander a boat and an atoll.

Native Americans:
You guys rock, I wish I was 'Throws rocks angrily'.

Americans:
Tell the truth I don't really have too much against these guys. I mean their foreign policy is s**t and all that, but they have never really done anything evil to New Zealand and I have not met any Americans I wanted to dissect with a cheese slice.

Australians:
The nose is not a speaking instrument.

White New Zealanders:
Every time someone in this country tries to do something well or puts themselves forward, the lot of you bunch together like a huddle of retarded white rabbits and discuss how bad, and 'up himself' the person is. You lot invented Tall poppy syndrome. You all think you are soooo laid back and relaxed, but you are all too damn scared to try anything big for fear of being shot down. We claim to be open minded and forward thinking but when something new presents itself we attempt with every once of our being to tear it down. Also be more impressed. Congratulate someone, not sit there in your useless reserved kiwi way going 'He could have done that better'.

Maori:
The past is not an excuse for your activities now. You want to make NZ one, stop trying to break it apart.

Indians:
I understand that in India you have a system where every price was up for negotiation. Well you see, if you cared to look around for five seconds you will notice something quite astounding. YOU ARE NOT IN INDIA, are you???! NO, do you see elephants? NO tigers either. That would probably be because you are in New Zealand. Don't try to haggle for every f****g thing. Also every single negotiation does not have to end with you ripping every cent out the hapless pleb on the other side of the bargaining table.

Have I missed anyone?

ROBERT MCNEIL on the Scots
The Scotsman

I can't believe these poor folk being inducted officially into British citizenship this week were made to sing 'God Save the Queen'. If they must sing something, why can't it be 'The Ace of Spades' (with associated head-banging movements) by Motorhead or, since England is after all Britain, *The Archers* theme tune?

In Scotland, they couldn't have 'Flower of Scotland', one of the least dirge – like anthems in the world, because of booing by our own Craven Scotch. So, what about Donald, 'Where's Yir Troosers'? Its pawky humour and kilt references would let newcomers know just where they'll stand – with the rest of us – in the United Kingdom settlement.

All week, debate has been raging – I speak loosely – about Polish people coming here to flippin' nirvana. I don't give a hoot even if, generally, I prefer population decline and like a lot of space. As long as folk are decent and nice and have got all their own teeth.

Scotland desperately needs people of different colours and physiognomies so that, with inter-marriage and whatnot, we can stop looking so ugly.

One thing, though, about people coming here: they must be willing to work. This is so that people like me, who are not willing to work, can get on with other things.

and *ANOTHER* thing...

JIM MCBETH on Scottishness
The Scotsman

I pondered the nature of Scottishness, and that sense of national identity which I have never experienced or aspired to.

I regard that appalling ditty 'Flower of Scotland' as a xenophobic dirge exemplifying all that is not good about the Scots.

I cannot embrace the ersatz rendering of my heritage. It has a lot to do with not having a big enough bottom. I'm revealing, here, sliding up the shutters on the dark night of the soul. The one (drunken) time I tried on a kilt it slipped over my nether region and fell to the floor.

Mercifully, I had not gone 'commando' so the disapprobation of my companions was confined only to the sartorial aspect of the episode. One of my chums viewed the sorry spectacle and opined: 'Jim, you need an a*** to be a Scot.'

But the deficiency of my non-Scottish bottom took time to get over. I just continue to thank God I was wearing pants.

CHARLES DICKENS on Washington
American Notes

As Washington may be called the head-quarters of tobacco-tinctured saliva, the time is come when I must confess, without any disguise, that the prevalence of those two odious practices of chewing and expectorating began about this time to be anything but agreeable, and soon became most offensive and sickening. In all the public places of America, this filthy custom is recognised.

122

In the courts of law, the judge has his spittoon, the crier his, the witness his, and the prisoner his; while the jurymen and spectators are provided for, as so many men who in the course of nature must desire to spit incessantly. In the hospitals, the students of medicine are requested, by notices upon the wall, to eject their tobacco juice into the boxes provided for that purpose, and not to discolour the stairs.

In public buildings, visitors are implored, through the same agency, to squirt the essence of their quids, or 'plugs', as I have heard them called by gentlemen learned in this kind of sweetmeat, into the national spittoons, and not about the bases of the marble columns.

But in some parts, this custom is inseparably mixed up with every meal and morning call, and with all the transactions of social life. The stranger, who follows in the track I took myself, will find it in its full bloom and glory, luxuriant in all its alarming recklessness, at Washington. And let him not persuade himself (as I once did, to my shame) that previous tourists have exaggerated its extent. The thing itself is an exaggeration of nastiness, which cannot be outdone.

ANNE ROBINSON on the Welsh
BBC's Room 101

The Welsh are always so pleased with themselves. I've never taken to them – what are they for? Nothing as far as I can understand. They are irritating and annoying and awful to look at.

We used to go on holiday and for day trips to Wales and they all spoke Welsh. Horrible.

JULIE BURCHILL on People who hate the Welsh
The Guardian

Without doubt the Welsh are the sexiest, best-looking and cleverest people in Europe, yet time and time again they let ignorant munters like Anne Robinson, AA Gill and Jeremy Clarkson wind them up. Yet just one look at any of this trio – Robinson with her sour little mug, Gill with a voice that makes me sound like Mariella Frostrup, or Clarkson, who single-handedly made blue jeans beyond the pale to youth, such is his repulsiveness – and you can tell immediately why they don't like the Welsh. Their bitching tells us nothing about the Welsh, and everything about them.

CHRISTOPHER HITCHENS on Moral Equivalence
The Atlantic Monthly

I take a trawl through my email and my mailbag...
Why sing the 'Battle Hymn of the Republic'? Don't they know John Brown was the first terrorist? ...
What about the civilian casualties in Vietnam, Guatemala, Gaza [fill in as necessary] ...?
This goes on all day, and it goes on while I sleep, so that I open a new batch each morning. Everyone writes to me as if he or she were bravely making a point for the very first time it had ever been made. And so I ask myself, in the spirit of self-criticism that I am enjoining upon these reflexive correspondents, whether I have any responsibility for this dismal tide of dreary traffic, this mob of pseudo-refugees taking shelter in half-baked moral equivalence.

6

If you ask me, people have got more money than sense...

FREDDIE WINDSOR on iPods

Artnik

Steve Jobs is a very clever man. He runs Apple, one of the biggest software companies in the world. He invented the Mac computer. He has just launched iTunes in Britain. Although Jobs is filthy rich already, his ambition is to become wealthier than Bill Gates. The iPod is part of his enrichment plan.

Last Christmas my parents, poor sods, gave me one. It cost them 400 big ones, and I was thrilled (not, let me add, at the cost – just the present). Like the two million or so other fools who found the same cubic box at the end of their stocking, I took this happy event to mean that for the rest of my life I could happily switch off into a cocoon-like dream world while this *i-Pod*, this miracle of modern science, this short white Hermes from another age, banged out endless tunes of my choice in the exact order I wanted.

'Made in California', the box read. Great!, I thought. Not, 'Made in the USA' or 'Carefully and lovingly assembled by under-paid elves in Lapland'. No. 'Made in California': this was an altogether superior guarantee of quality, one which surely meant my new toy was somehow impervious to the ills which plague lesser items of machinery. Not for Apple's iPod the soul-sapping ache of the desktop crash; not for Steve Jobs's new product the unsolvable nightmare of the blue TV screen. This was going to change my life.

I suspected there might be a catch – even the most seemingly perfect appliance can let you down, as anyone who has ever suffered the misery of opening a Breville toaster to find half of their sandwich stuck to the top will tell you. The big *if*, of course, with all Walkman-type gadgets is battery life. If they are battery hogs, then they eat away at your pocket as well as your peace of mind. But the iPod seemed fine. It had a rechargeable and on page 43 of the user's manual there is this pledge from Apple: 'A fully charged battery provides about *8 hours* [my italics] of playing time.'

Oh yeah? No, it doesn't. In my case, it lasts for forty minutes on a bad day; perhaps just over an hour on a good one. Put it this way: it takes me half an hour to get to work in the morning, when I generally like to use my iPod (retail price, just to recap, of £400). If I use it again at lunchtime while I'm reading the paper, I know for certain that if I turn it on again after work the thing will be deader than the deadest dodo or red squirrel.

But Apple are the good guys, remember. This isn't Microsoft – the baddies. If Microsoft said 8 hours and you got one, you would not complain nor would you be surprised. You'd think, 'That's Microsoft for you.'

If you ask me, people have got more money than sense...

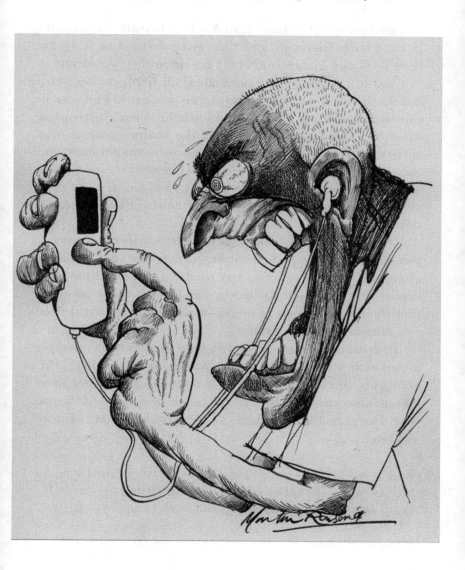

Maybe we should hand it to Apple. They are going head-to-head with Microsoft and they have decided to stoop to their level and blatantly f****** lie about their products.

And it's not just this about the iPod that gets my goat; it's the WAY it packs up that drives me mad. The way it just switches itself off in the middle of a song without a word of explanation, even when the battery icon in the corner looks two thirds full, and when you turn it back on, guess what? – it's suddenly completely empty.

Hang on, though, what's this? A message. Good news, perhaps? 'No more battery power remains. Please connect iPod to power.'

Oh, no more POWER remains, eh? Connect to power, you say? F*** you, what the hell do you mean, I've been charging you for days, you little bastard. Note the maddening omission of 'the' or 'an', as if Apple assumes that their contraption is somehow such a good friend that you are on first-name terms.

It's reached the stage where I view the whole business as a personal stand-off between me and the iPod. It's the arrogance of the thing – if I ever meet the guy responsible for making my day-to-day life such a misery, I know what I'm going to do to him. It involves my iPod. And it will hurt.

The Letter I Would Love To Write
Bazman:JustRamIt.co.uk

Dear Sir/Madam,

Whilst I imagine you expect to have sent a shiver down my spine with your threat of never buying the products of the company I work for again, I regret to inform you, and this may come as a surprise, but I don't give a f***.

My employer is the biggest manufacturer of said product in the world and guess what? – they don't give a f*** either. If they gave a f***, then they would have a better after-sales service in place and I wouldn't have to listen to whiny pantpissers like you every day growing indignant over the loss of your porn stash.

My employer shifts so many units that he benefits from a thing called economies of scale, which lowers the price of the product – and sometimes the quality. Consequently, things break, especially if you buy cheap things, because some wheeler-dealer computer salesman is trading on the reputation of the manufacturer (my employer) who, in order to achieve economies of scale, is using cheaper materials, but don't tell anyone I told you that.

Also, you tragic techie turd tail, you didn't buy the f***** thing from my employer, you bought it from some high street retailer/supermarket chain or market stall/friend who ripped you off.

At least if you had the cop-on to go to a legitimate retailer, you are entitled to some kind of after-sales service (whether they say you do or do not, it's actually statutory law), but if you really do expect to get a quality product from 'some bloke at a market', then you are an idiot and you deserve whatever s*** you get.

Also, I am not pummelled into submission by your threat to take the case to trading standards. Take the case to Trading Standards and, if you have any joy, please let me know. I would love to not have to listen to you and your limp-wristed, quivering-in-a-darkened-room-surroundedby-encrusted-kleenex-before-your-giant-c***splash-smeared-plasma-screen ilk prattling on about the poor quality products my employer manufacturers and the appallingly bad after-sales service. I know about it. I'm here every day and you are not the first ever person to call me up with a defective product, you moron. If trading standards can help you, then they also help me. Do it. Do it now and call me back because I want to know. (They never call me back...sometimes I feel so lonely and disappointed).

Next, why are you making me repeat myself? Why? Why? Did you not listen to what I said? Was I speaking some obscure dialect? I am no linguist, Noam Chomsky I am not! – but I am reasonably articulate and know perfectly well how to explain the procedures involved in our employee-customer relationship to intellectually indigent dolts like yourself, as I do it umpteen times a day. I can do it with my eyes closed, with one arm behind my back, without even thinking. I even deliver it in dead-pan monotone similar to your own primeval grunting in order not to confuse you, sir.

Finally, I thank you for your call/letter/fax/e-mail, it has truly, inestimably enriched my otherwise mundane day but tragically this communication must come to an end. I have outlined all services available and also those that are not available and no amount of cajoling, complaining or that weird, bestial whimpering thing your voice is doing is going to reverse the aforementioned order. I have provided ways and means that you can avail yourself of these other services, truly my duty to you is at an end. I am not your friend, nor am I your servant. I am an anonymous stranger and I bade you have a nice day.

What Technical Support is really thinking
JustRamIt.co.uk

PS: Never mind all that s***. Here's the truth: I don't care. I really don't. I am not a career man. I am what is in the employment market referred to as a 'bottom feeder'. I am the first line of support. I am the unkempt, unshaven, drug abusing, alcoholic, black sheep of the family, can't hold a job down, can't fashion a decent relationship call centre operative of your nightmares. However, I – unlike you – speak several languages and can operate a computer. HA! HA !
The irony is thick, I know; but not as thick as you.

I don't have to care. I have no future, no offspring, no mortgage, no ties, no love – nothing. I am horribly lonely from Monday to Friday, 9-5pm but as soon as 5pm comes, I get a rush of adrenalin like you can't imagine because I know that soon I will be drunk or stoned with not a care in the world.
It gets worse.

I chose this lifestyle. I don't have to be this. I could be you. I'm in the same tax bracket as you but nothing is more anathema to me than to be like you so I linger malignantly here in between you and what you desire, and act simultaneously as facilitator and preventer as is my whim and, when we die, you from your ulcer or stress induced cancer and me from heart disease or liver failure, we will both kneel before the same God or rot in the same soil and leave nothing but the enormous pile of faulty goods we have collectively accumulated.

and *ANOTHER* thing...

GROUCHO MARX to Elgin American Compacts
The Groucho Letters: Letters from and to Groucho Marx

Dear Mr.G.,

You could have knocked me over with a compact when one of your hirelings arrived here last week with a solid gold watch in his hands. My previous sponsors sold gasoline, corn flakes and beer. These, needless to say, have a value, but how would a man look walking around with a bottle of beer tied to his wrist?

The watch is a thing of beauty, and will be a joy forever, and I would have thanked you sooner, but I purposely waited a week, for I wanted to make sure the lousy thing would run.

In 1948, Groucho Marx wrote a letter to Warner Brothers stating his opinion about trademarks. Warner Brothers released the film *Casablanca* in 1943 and wanted to prevent the Marx Brothers from calling one of their pictures *A Night in Casablanca*.

The Groucho Letters

Dear Warner Brothers,

Apparently there is more than one way of conquering a city and holding it as your own. For example, up to the time that we contemplated making this picture, I had no idea that the city of Casablanca belonged exclusively to Warner Brothers. However, it was only a few days after our announcement appeared that we received your long, ominous legal document warning us not to use the name Casablanca.

It seems that in 1471, Ferdinand Balboa Warner, your great-great-grandfather, while looking for a shortcut to the city of Burbank, had stumbled on the shores of Africa and, raising his alpenstock (which he later turned in for a hundred shares of the common), named it Casablanca.

I just don't understand your attitude. Even if you plan on re-releasing your picture, I am sure that the average movie fan could learn in time to distinguish between Ingrid Bergman and Harpo. I don't know whether I could, but I certainly would like to try.

You claim you own Casablanca and that no one else can use that name without your permission. what about 'Warner Brothers'? Do you own that, too? You probably have the right to use the name Warner, but what about Brothers? Professionally, we were brothers long before you were. We were touring the sticks as the Marx Brothers when Vitaphone was still a gleam in the inventor's eye, and even before us there had been other brothers – the Smith Brothers; the Brothers Karamazov; Dan Brothers, an outfielder with Detroit; and 'Brother, Can You Spare a Dime?' (This was originally 'Brothers, Can You Spare a Dime?' but this was spreading a dime pretty thin, so they threw out one brother gave all the money to the other one and whittled it down to, 'Brother, Can You Spare a Dime?').

Now Jack, how about you? Do you maintain that yours is an original name? Well, it's not. It was used long before you were born. Offhand, I can think of two Jacks – there was Jack of 'Jack and the Beanstalk', and Jack the Ripper, who cut quite a figure in his day.

As for you, Harry, you probably sign your checks, sure in the belief that you are the first Harry of all time and that all other Harrys are impostors. I can think of two Harrys that preceded you. There was Lighthouse Harry of Revolutionary fame and a Harry Appelbaum who lived on the corner of 93rd Street and Lexington Avenue. Unfortunately, Appelbaum wasn't too well known. The last I heard of him, he was selling neckties at Weber and Heilbroner.

Now about Burbank studio. I believe this is what you brothers call your place. Old man Burbank is gone. Perhaps you remember him. He was a great man in the garden. His wife often said Luther had ten green thumbs. What a witty woman she must have been! Burbank was the wizard who crossed all those fruits and vegetables until he had the poor plants in such a confused and jittery condition that they could never decide whether to enter the dining room on the meat platter or the dessert dish.

This is pure conjecture, of course, but who knows — perhaps Burbank's survivors aren't too happy with the fact that a plant that grinds out pictures on a quota settled in their town, appropriated Burbank's name and uses it as a front for their films. It is even possible that the Burbank family is prouder of the potato produced by the old man than they are of the fact that from your studio emerged *Casablanca* or even *Gold Diggers of 1931*.

This all seems to add up to a pretty bitter tirade, but I assure you it's not meant to. I love Warners. Some of my best friends are Warner Brothers. It is even possible that I am doing you an injustice and that you, yourselves, know nothing at all about this dog-in-the-Wanger attitude. It wouldn't surprise me at all to discover that the heads of your legal department are unaware of this absurd dispute, for I am acquainted with many of them and they are fine fellows with curly black hair, double-breasted suits and a love of their fellow man that out-Saroyans Saroyan.

I have a hunch that this attempt to prevent us from using the title is the brainchild if some ferret-faced shyster, serving a brief apprenticeship in your legal department. I know the type well – hot out of law school, hungry for success and too ambitious to follow the natural laws of promotion. This bar sinister probably needled your attorneys, most of whom are fine fellows with curly black hair, double-breasted suits, etc., into attempting to enjoin us. Well, he won't get away with it! We'll fight him to the highest court! No pasty-faced legal adventurer is going to cause bad blood between the Warners and the Marxes. We are all brothers under the skin and we'll remain friends till the last reel of *A Night in Casablanca* goes tumbling over the spool.

How can I help?
John McVicar: Artnik

A lot of large firms are 'outsourcing' their call centres to places like India and Bangladesh. Obviously to save money, it is certainly nothing to do with a touching desire on behalf of BT or Norwich Union to employ Indians or Bangladeshis because the members of their boards love the Indian subcontinent. Is there a thriving market in luxury holiday villas for western executives in the Bay of Bengal?

But large companies are in a cutthroat market and they have to reduce costs in order to fund golden handshakes to executives, back-handers to union leaders, and pay for higher management to go to exotic locations for pep-up courses on how to become an 'indispensable employee in a dispensable world'.

They do a bit of company bonding on the side too. Incidentally, they never go to Bangladesh, it's too far, too hot, and Dhaka's blue light district is plagued by power

135

cuts and AIDS.

Dhaka does do call centres though, even though most of those answering calls from England can't understand basic English. In case you think this is a racist statistic can I add that there's a pretty huge chunk of English Caucasians who can't speak or understand basic English either. It's true that most of them have been cretinised by listening to rap music and its derivatives. They like mind-rot noise – don't they know it's Afro-America's revenge for the slave trade?

But why do the morons who train our Dhaka call centre drones tell them to answer every call with 'How can I help?' Well, that's after they have told you their first name. When you ask for their surname – because you know that you'll need it when you make your complaint about their incompetence – they tell you that they are 'forbeeden to give our full name'. However, before they field your enquiry they give you the third degree. Never mind your surname, they want to know when you last downloaded some porn from 'Underage Sluts'.

Another number that they pull is to get you on first name terms. 'May I call you John?'

'No, you must call me Mister Schwarzkopf.'

'But Jo... Mr Sarcof... your name is Mc..'

'Don't insult my mother. Her name is Schwarzkopf and everyone calls me that even though my official name is the one I just interrupted you mispronouncing. My father was English and in a primogeniture society, like England, the children of a marriage take the name of the father. But the name that I use and which everyone knows me by is Schwarzkopf. And will you please learn to pronounce it correctly. I don't care about my father's surname but my mother's – God bless her soul – is a very distinguished

German name, her father was a Colonel in the Waffen-SS and died fighting for his country and the Fuhrer. Schwarzkopf means blackhead in English. We were always told not to squeeze ours but, of course, we did. It is one of the pleasures of adolescence to have blackheads, squeeze them, then watch and feel them slide out like a penis from its sheath. What blackhead means in Bangldeshi I have no idea and I suspect you do not either. Do you, Deeba?'

You can run like this and Dhaka Deeba will be quite happy to listen and play along. Again she is instructed to do just that. By now you should be smelling the rat that has crawled up your a***hole to die and is decaying in your lower colon. Because, yes, you have gone down the exact same road that I have. We all have.

So what is gong on? Well, the big corporations with a large lower-class client base, such as car insurance and telecommunications, realised a few years ago that their customer relations were increasingly dealing with hordes of irrelevant inquiries. People who really just wanted a chat were ringing up with contrived inquires in order to talk about last night's episode of *Coronation Street*. It was costing a bomb, even with boneheads on check-out counter wages.

The first attempt to solve this problem was to design automatic telephone answering systems that were interactive. You know those lists of options and sub-menus that take you round and round until you end up where you started and give up. Well, that is after you have listened to a pre-recorded warning that 'this conversation may be recorded for training purposes'.

Let me tell you a secret: these conversations are never,

ever recorded for training purposes. There is no training for the nitwits who skulk behind these systems. Why do they need any training? All they are instructed to do is tell any inquirer, who by fluke or some glitch in the system gets through to them, that their question or request is dealt with by another department and they must ring 'this number' (they then give you the number of another interactive answering system that takes you on the same merry-go-round).

However, this also proved counter-productive as even the witless idiots who don't do their business by Internet or mail realised they were being given the finger and began ringing company headquarters to complain.

Some genius in customer relations came up with the answer to it all: 'Look, they want to talk to a real person. So we will give them a real person...in Dhaka, who will work for less than it takes to feed your dog. Give them a computer screen, a telephone and an Internet connection and work them 12 hours a day. That'll solve it.'

It did. And it has become another curse of living in England in the 21st century. Roll on global warming, the melting of the polar ice-caps and a rise in sea levels. They reckon that a 5 centimetres rise will do for Dhaka nicely.

Meanwhile, get back at these call centre cretins. Anyone who answers your call with 'How can I help?' say to them: 'That really does beg the question. How could some unemployable f***wit like you possibly help anyone. You can't even even help yourself, otherwise you would be on the first banana boat to England and not giving me grief from a call centre in Dhaka.'

7

It's changed, innit, this country – for the worse

CAR OWNER on parking wardens
Artnik

Everyone hates parking wardens. But there's a reason. They are Satan's representatives on earth. They cannot be bargained with. They cannot be stopped. They breed.

The mean streets are crawling with them. They meet on corners and discuss their latest kill. They can't speak English, or they pretend not to, in order to avoid the difficult emotional questions regularly asked of them by law-abiding citizens who simply want to know what the hell they think they're doing with their sorry little lives.

But it's not the Daleks who actually patrol our cities that we should really reserve our hate for. It's the people who give them their uniforms - and take most of our money. And it's the councils, who absolve themselves of any moral burden by syndicating the responsibility out to private companies who aren't accountable to voters and don't give a damn.

Sure, SOMEONE has to make sure our streets are relatively uncluttered, that residents have priority, that city central traffic is regulated and no-one gets hemmed in. And it should be an elected body answerable to its citizens. But those same tinpot tyrants get fed up of making unpopular decisions, and instead auction off the right to arbitrarily tax the general public whenever they see fit. Which means they profit (without responsibility) and the private firms profit (without accountability). The only possible way this adds up is if the punters get charged twice.

That's why the charges have shot up recently. That's why they increase exponentially over and over again while you debate whether or not you should humour the bastards by actually paying. And that's why clampers patrol the roads – so they can hit you with the double whammy. Because they've paid for that filthy contract and they're damn well going to make sure it's lucrative.

These clamp-happy parasites tend to be on the payroll of different scamsters again. They follow around behind the footsoldiers in their vans, like kerb-crawlers looking for ass. Like ambulance chasers. And when you're down, they kick you in the teeth by causing criminal damage to your wheels. Why is this fair or necessary when you've already been punished? It isn't. Where is the logic as to who receives this additional super-charge and massive inconvenience? There is none – again, it's totally arbitrary. It tends to be just the first few people they come across with yellow tickets in their windshield, regardless of the nature or seriousness of their offence – regardless of whether or

not they're actually inconveniencing other road-users, and how long they're supposed to have gone over their time. Then they repeat the cowardly duck-shoot until they run out of their horrid yellow jaws.

There is no appeals process with clamping. It doesn't matter if there was an administrative error, by human hand or by faulty machine, in the distribution of the ticket. Once you have a clamp in place, utterly disabling YOUR privately-owned vehicle, your only option is to ring the cackling cash-goblins who put it there...and ring them at your expense, too.

They will then come round as and when they see fit – they will give you an unhelpful prediction between 20 minutes and three hours. They cannot be more specific, so in that period you must wait by your vehicle or miss your chance of freedom. Note that this will always happen on a weekday, during working hours – YOUR working hours. And you will have to pay up on the spot, without legal representation, without the time to organise your finances and take out the punitive loan you will probably need to ship the blow.

This is illegal. Well, only technically – only by the wider statutes of justice that are the foundation of this free land. In practice they can do it, they do do it, and they do it with the blessing of those who are elected to protect us.

So blame the traffic wardens who become goose-stepping agents of darkness the moment they put on a uniform. Blame them because there were other choices they could have made to make money, choices with more human dignity, like undertaking or street-sweeping.

Blame the companies who care more about money than human rights, inventors of a new breed of 'customers' –

unwilling captives roped in by stealth. They give those people the uniform that turns them into monsters, and then pay them by commission 'per hit' to encourage trigger-happy ticket-slapping. They run the production line that turns harmless, small-minded idiots into power-crazed fiends, who can grant jurisdiction over generally more evolved, moral and public-spirited citizens. They add to the huge financial burden on the already-beleaguered motorist, stripping him bare and buggering him backwards.

And blame the local councils, the people with nominal control of the roads. People we voted in to serve the public good. They didn't want that responsibility so they sold it on. And they gave an undemocratic body of thieves and charlatans the power to tax us.

But then again, big fish like governments and corporations are notoriously hard to get at – so if you prefer just take it out on the little people in the black and yellow. The road-wasps, if you will. The public face of evil.

Here's a good scheme. Come up behind them on the streets and knock off their hats. When they complain, say you're just doing your job. When they ask you to pick it up, explain patiently that the hat's already on the pavement, and there's nothing you can do about it now. Stealing a copper's tit-hat IS a criminal offence- but it's not really assault to knock off a civilian's headpiece, providing it's not of religious significance. This is where you can best remind them that, contrary to appearance, they are not in fact the police.

Whatever you do, don't blame yourself for where you parked. Always blame them... Remember *ALWAYS*.

SIMON JENKINS on Traffic Wardens]
Evening Standard

We have the nonsense of a London of rundown estates, scruffy parks, ill-swept pavements and understaffed libraries, while hundreds of traffic wardens (400 in Westminster alone) 'tax farm' the gutters. They collect money which can be spent only on restlessly digging up roads and pavements and installing lights, speed bumps and cycle lanes.

The next round of this madness is for many speed bumps to be removed and replaced by even more expensive speed cameras, latest toy of the taxing classes. This is demented public administration, typical of this Government.

Whatever happened to Mr Darling's 'holes czars', invented in November 2002 as a headline gimmick? Roadworks in central London are back to their worst ways of old.

MARK BOLLAND on Traffic Wardens
News of the World

From my kitchen window I can see a betting shop. Drivers stop for five minutes on a single yellow line while they pop in to put a bet on. Traffic wardens wait around the corner, out of sight in packs of three, to swoop and give parking tickets.

Why? Did any of us ever vote for this to happen? Do the arrogant idiots in charge of all this care what we think? Of course they don't.

I'm in dispute with my local authority, Islington in

London, about council tax. They owe me £600 but say I owe THEM £300! They threatened me with court action so I thought I'd do the same to them. I'll let you know how I get on. But if that traffic warden policy is anything to go by, I'll be pounced on by at least three lawyers:

One to provide the red tape, another to tie us up in it and a third to mail a vast bill for their efforts.

RICHARD SUSSKIND on Speed Cameras
Gresham college

I once had a nasty experience of speed cameras and I may never be the same again. Let me be clear from the outset – using speed cameras to reduce death and injuries on the road is a good thing. No question. But what exasperates me is putting them in accident-free areas, as seems to be happening more and more. Indeed, if I may launch into a tangential rant, I find such speed cameras only marginally less annoying than the draconian penalty regime that underpins the Congestion Charge or the use of private contractors for clamping wrongly parked vehicles. Both of these schemes seem to be much more about raising funds than managing our thoroughfares.

Back to my experience. Several years ago, on the morning of my 40th birthday in fact, nestling in the small pile of greetings cards, I found a communication that did not bring good tidings. It was a notice of intended prosecution, alleging that at 10.58 on 16th March 2001 I had been driving in Oxford at 38 mph in a 30 mph limit. Hardly a heinous felony, I felt, but I resolved in the spirit of the day to take the penalty on the chin. The following

145

day, a second notice arrived, this time bearing the allegation that at 11.01 on 16th March, I had been travelling at 40 mph in a 30 mph zone (although a different road from the first incident). I was heading for the award of six penalty points in around 3 minutes. I was seething (and still am).

I completed the relevant forms, conceding that I had been the driver at the time of the incidents (and ignoring the guidance of two well-meaning lawyer friends who advised of almost foolproof, but dodgy, ways of avoiding the charges). But I did ask, in writing, if the police might let me know if such circumstances are treated as distinct incidents or as one incident. I said that I would want to argue that the two events, given they were so close together, should be treated as a single event. After all, I went on, if a car was travelling over the limit for a period of, say, a minute, and its speed was ascertained every ten seconds, then while it could be said that six offences had occurred, that would surely seem rather bizarre. I knew this was not the finest of legal arguments but I felt it was worth running and certainly worth a reply, which I did not get (and how infuriating is that?) until I sent a reminder. When the response did come, it was not sympathetic. It was dismissive in the manner of so many standard form letters and raised my blood pressure well above the hypertension danger line. To underline the thrust of his retort, the responding bureaucrat sent two copies of the letter, identical but for the different file references for each incident. This was a nice touch, legally, and one which no doubt afforded the author some considerable satisfaction. It wound me up yet further.

Incidentally, the legislation which I was said to have

contravened was cryptically referred to in all communications as "RTRA 1984". What is the average Joe meant to make of that? Could it not be spelled out in full? In the event, having chatted through my case and the "RTRA 1984" with various practising and academic lawyers, magistrates and police officers, I resolved to accept the offer of 6 penalty points (thus sullying my clean licence) and a fine of £120. I remain bitter and twisted about the incident (note - not incidents).

Prior to this brush with criminal justice, my last contact with the system (other than as a regular adviser to it) had been eighteen months previously when, some time during one night, while I was upstairs with my wife and three young children, our house was burgled. Blessedly unaware that there had been intruders, we awoke to find various valuables had been removed and loaded into our car which had also been taken. A couple of months later, just outside my house, a young thug (under the influence of something or other) drove his car directly at me and my neighbour. We were lucky to escape serious injury. On both occasions, the initial police response was friendly and sympathetic but any later inquiries about the progress of the investigation were met with lacklustre, pessimistic, defeatist and even intolerant response, as though any such loss or event should be written off as inevitable, much like the bad debts that any business expects to incur each year. No closure whatsoever. But good fuel for regular, random ranting.

Nor has there been successful apprehension of the villains who recently held a lady at knife point in our pleasant English village; nor of the men who tried to mug one of my sons. Current statistics may suggest an overall

147

decline in crime across the country but in my neck of the woods, the widespread feeling is that crime, especially against the person and property, is rising alarmingly.

When it comes to speed cameras, here is the nub: the systematic and efficient pursuit of largely law-abiding citizens who have committed minor motoring offences contrasts starkly with my own experience of the pursuit of serious criminals. It is galling to be so competently and mercilessly convicted – twice within a few minutes – for marginally exceeding the speed limit late one evening, when various assaults on my family and home pass virtually unnoticed.

Introducing speed cameras in accident-free areas while failing to control violence and burglary is like tidying the deck chairs on the Titanic. It serves to alienate citizens rather than enjoin them to help in fighting crime. It creates a tension between people and the police at a time when we should all be working together in community-based measures to counter blatant anti-social behaviour. Initiatives such as Neighbourhood Watch should flourish in our current times of need and not be regarded cynically as taxpayers doing the job of police, thus releasing the latter to focus on minor road offences.

I understand speed cameras are now being proposed for our village – at locations, to my knowledge, that have not been the scenes of any injuries, still less fatalities. Meanwhile, as said, serious crime is on the increase here. If we are putting in cameras, they should surely be CCTV devices and not speed cameras – to help pinpoint serious offenders and not generally law-abiding citizens.
I rest my rant.

SIMON JENKINS on trains:
Evening Standard

Sometimes technological nemesis is delicious. I was recently journeying on the 'toffee-nosed' Bournemouth line out of Waterloo. Its plutocratic customers have been endlessly indulged by successive rail companies with new rolling stock, while the plebs on the South-Eastern division took its cast-offs, known as 'cascades'. I was looking forward to sampling South-Western's latest on-board info-terminal and digitised latte machine.

Then I was told that a computer glitch somewhere near Clapham had led to 'train failure'. Replacement stock was on the way.

The next thing I saw made my eyes mist over. A slam door rattled and wheezed into the Waterloo platform. London Bridge had come to the rescue.

It was like a ghost train out of *Brief Encounter*. It was a dosser with a mug of tea come to rescue the victims of a power failure at the Ritz.

These trains run as if by magic, with their driving cabs apparently missing from the front. The paintwork is filthy, the upholstery lacerated and stitched. Corridors stink of a thousand football specials.

Light bulbs and coat hooks have long gone to furnish some lonely Southwark bedsit. Old curtains reek of coal dust. The heating is ferocious in summer and non-existent in winter. I expect to see Holmes and Watson crouching in the corners, mice scurrying beneath their feet.

Worst, or best, are the windows, embedded still in wooden frames. The grime should be listed as historic. The sheen of red brake dust that coats the coach exterior coagulates into rust around the window glass, dripping with condensation. The passing Weald is thus seen as if through a Victorian sepia picture frame. I am told that these windows can only be cleaned with a razor blade, which is why they remain dirty.

South West Trains said that it was unreasonable to expect new trains to be as reliable as old ones, because they are more complicated and 'there is so much more to go wrong'. That is the future of public transport in a nutshell.'

Western Morning Press
Crap Towns

Inverness is so bleak that even the pigeons look depressed. The buildings are so grim they look like they're in mourning. It always rains, and the bitter cold wind has chiselled the locals' faces into a narrow sulk. What do they do for fun on a Saturday night – skin rabbits? I went there once for a wedding and we all got riotously drunk. But then, what else is there to do in Inverness except to slug whisky by the beer glass and curse the English?

Crap Towns II lists the top 100 most undesirable places to live.

One of those not mentioned is Hartlepool, famous for hanging a monkey the natives mistook for a Frenchman. But that's probably because no one in Hartlepool can read.

Instead, the unlikely chart-toppers include places such as Bath, Oxford and Windsor.

Bath, according to one contributor, is: 'Essentially a

retirement town with an unpleasant amount of students. The centre of this beautiful city is a concrete trench lined with McDonald's restaurants and vicious teenagers playing with lock knives. In the summer it fills to the brim with loud tourists who clog the narrow streets like the coagulated grease in a Scotsman's arteries. Then there's snooty Windsor where women over 60 'lose the plot altogether and convince themselves they actually are the Queen'. And this gem: 'Imagine exams to find the most odious individuals in the South East and all those who pass with flying colours were sent to Brighton.'

Let me volunteer my own nominations because, as a well-traveled man, I have lived or lingered in a few places that some 'friendly bombs' could only upgrade.

First up is Blackpool where my beloved and I visited in a spirit of irony. We managed to evade the escaped convict on the train but there was no escaping the B&Bs. We got a room where we were kept awake all night by what sounded like a Boeing taking off. It was the lift. Breakfast was microwaved 'bacon' curled up at the ends, and grease with an egg on top. The waiter looked like he hadn't had a wash since he was christened. Gina had taken her posh frock and I my three-piece suit because we fancied a spin in the Tower Ballroom. It was closed, and three days before the season started the only other people in town were 3,000 Nora Battys from the Inner Wheel. In the first pub we visited the locals stared at us because we looked as if we'd been fed. In the second a crazed drunk woman mistook me for a priest and started praying. The best souvenir of Blackpool is the memory of why you won't go back.

Next is Benwell in Newcastle, a vipers' nest of so many burglars that they have run out of neighbours' houses to burn out. The kids will mug you for your bag of chips. The dogs go round in packs for protection. I lived in this war zone for two years and it almost made me sentimental about west Belfast.

Then there's charming Durham, immortalised in song by Roger Whittaker but more obviously crawling with thousands of toff students – too thick to go anywhere else – who ponce around looking like rejects from *Brideshead Revisited*.

And what list could do without Grantham, which gave us Margaret Thatcher, and where people gather round the war memorial for something to look at.

Or venturing down to the West country, the yoghurt-weavers' capital of England – Totnes. It may be pretty and historic, but modern Totnes exists so that spirit healers and crystal gazers don't have to join a Jobseekers scheme. They have somewhere to live among the only people who don't think they are space cadets – other spacers. It's the only town in England where grown men who dress like Geoffrey out of Rainbow and do 'drumming' are the norm. It's the only town in England where not looking like Geoffrey out of Rainbow marks you as an outsider.

And thence to fair Plymouth, my adopted home and a wonderful place with the glaring exception of the city centre. Granted, Mr Hitler had something to do with this. But who let Stalin's architects experiment on the place for 50 years? The central-point of this great city is a finger of sheet metal called the Sundial where grungy teenagers with 'attitude' hunch together to compare acne. When my dad – a retired welder/plater – saw it, he said it looked like it was

in transit from the factory. I once had the misfortune to
arrive by mistake at night in Katowice, the grimmest city in
Poland. Or was it Plymouth city centre – I get confused.

DAVID ROBSON on English Seaside Towns
The Express

Ludicrous as it may seem, Blackpool businessmen have
launched a campaign to stop traders on the seafront from
selling such tacky gifts as plastic bottoms and rude tee
shirts. They think it's time they raised the tone of the
place. Have they gone stark raving bonkers?

For heaven's sake, what do they think is the point of
Blackpool?

Why was it, and why should it always be the greatest
place in Lancashire, England, Europe, the World and
possibly the Universe?

Because it is dead common. What do they want on the
Golden Mile?

Antiquarian book shops? Poetry readings? String
quartets? Bijou stalls selling tiny organic truffle soufflés
subtly flavoured with lemongrass and drizzled with extra
virgin olive oil? They'll be wanting to take down Blackpool
Tower next because it's too much of a phallic symbol.

'Blackpool is pretty quiet,' says Bob Cotton of the
British Hospitality Association, 'but the Lake District is
bursting at the seams.' Have we all gone stupid? The whole
point of the Lake District is that there's not supposed to be
anybody there.

And what we do like about Britain are the posh bits, the

genteel. There can be nowhere in the land more genteel than Frinton-on-Sea in Essex where the locals recently fought a pitched battle against the opening of a fish-and-chip shop and another about the opening of a pub.

In the Thirties the architect Oliver Hill, who wanted to create an Essex version of fashionable Deauville across the Channel, wrote: 'To create a similar atmosphere here involves, first and foremost, the elimination of the vulgar plebs. . . there must be nothing to attract day trippers.'

He was too aware of the unspeakably horrible seaside fun that millions from London enjoyed in nearby Southend.

The successful British holiday these days is the one that makes the elements irrelevant – the country house hotel, the resort-cum-fitness centre, the gourmet establishment, the reading group weekend... Torbay may be suffering but suave Salcombe is very much in demand.

Many of those who holiday at the English seaside nowadays are simply too rich to bother to go abroad, or so rich that they holiday at their own little place here before going abroad.'

TOBIAS SMOLLETT on London
Humphrey Clinker[1771]

What temptation can a man of my turn and temperament have, to live in a place where every corner teems with fresh objects of detestation and disgust? What kind of taste and organs must those people have, who really prefer the adulterate enjoyments of the town to the genuine pleasures of a country retreat? Most people, I know, are originally seduced by vanity, ambition, and childish curiosity; which cannot be gratified, but in the busy haunts of men: but, in the course of this gratification, their very organs of sense are perverted, and they become habitually lost to every sense of what is genuine and excellent in its own nature.

I am pent up in frowzy lodgings, where there is not room enough to swing a cat; and I breath the steams of endless putrefaction; and these would, undoubtedly, produce a pestilence, if they were not qualified by the gross acid of sea-coal, which is itself a pernicious nuisance to lus of any delicacy of texture: but even this boasted corrector cannot prevent those languid, sallow looks, that distinguish the inhabitants of London from those ruddy swains that lead a country-life – I go to bed after midnight, jaded and restless from the dissipations of the day – I start every hour from my sleep, at the horrid noise of the watchman bawling the hour through every street, and thundering at every door; a set of useless fellows, who serve no other purpose except that of disturbing the repose of the inhabitants; and by five o' clock I start out of bed, in consequence of the still more dreadful alarm made by the country carts, and noisy rustics bellowing green pease beneath my window. If I would drink water, I must quaff the maukish contents of an open aqueduct, exposed to all manner of defilement; or swallow that which comes from the river Thames, impregnated with all the filth of London and Westminster – Human excrement is the least offensive part of the concrete, which is composed of all the drugs, minerals and poisons, used in mechanics and manufacture, enriched with the putrefying carcases of beasts and men; and mixed with the scourings of all the washtubs, kennels, and common sewers, within the bills of humanity. This is the agreeable potation, extolled by the Londoners, as the finest water in the universe.

The bread I eat in London, is a deleterious paste, mixed up with chalk, alum, and bone-ashes; insipid to the taste and destructive to the constitution. The good people are not ignorant of this adulteration; but they prefer it to wholesome bread, because it is whiter than the meal of corn: thus they sacrifice their taste and their health, and the lives of their tender infants, to the most absurd gratification of a misjudging eye; and the miller, or the baker, is obliged to poison them and their families, in order to live by his profession. The same monstrous depravity appears in their veal, which is bleached by repeated bleedings, and other villainous arts, till there is not a drop of juice left in the body, and the poor animal is paralytic before it dies; so void of all taste, nourishment, and savour, that a man might dine as comfortably on a white fricassee of kid-skin gloves; or chip hats from Leghorn.

Perhaps, you will hardly believe they would be so mad as to boil their greens with brass halfpence, in order to improve their colour; and yet nothing is more true. Indeed, without this improvement in the colour, they have no personal merit. They are produced in an artificial soil, and taste of nothing but the dunghills, from whence they spring.

Of the fish, I need say nothing in this hot weather, but that it comes sixty, seventy, fourscore, and a hundred miles by land-carriage; a circumstance sufficient, without any comment, to turn a Dutchman's stomach, even if his nose were not saluted in every alley by the sweet savour of fresh mackarel kept in slime-pits. The green colour, so much admired by the voluptuaries of this metropolis, is occasioned by the vitriolic scum, which rises on the surface of the stagnant and stinking water.

In Covent Garden, little else but the refuse of the market falls to the share of the community, and that is distributed by such filthy hands, as I cannot look at without loathing. It was not but yesterday that I saw a dirty barrow-bunter in the street, cleaning her dusty fruit with her own spittle; and who knows but some fine lady of St. James's parish might admit into her delicate mouth those very cherries, which had been rolled and moistened between the filthy, and, perhaps, ulcerated chops of a St. Giles's huckster – I need not dwell upon the pallid, contaminated mash, which they call strawberries; soiled and tossed by geasy paws through twenty baskets crusted with dirt; and then presented with the worst milk, thickened with the worst flour, into a bad likeness of cream: but the milk itself should not pass unanalysed, the produce of faded cabbage-leaves and sour draff, lowered with hot water, frothed with bruised snails, carried through the streets in open pails, exposed to foul rinsings, discharged from doors and windows, spittle, snot, and tobacco-quids from foot passengers, overflowings from mud carts, spatterings from coach wheels, dirt and trash chucked into it by roguish boys for the joke's sake, the spewings of infants, who have slabbered in the tin-measure, which is thrown back in that condition among the milk, for the benefit of the next customer; and, finally, the vermin that drops from the rags of the nasty drab that vends this precious mixture, under the respectable denomination of milk-maid.

I shall conclude this catalogue of London dainties, with

that table beer, guiltless of hops and malt, vapid and nauseous; much fitter to facilitate the operations of a vomit, than to quench thirst and promote digestion; the tallowy, rancid mass, called butter, manufactured with candle grease and kitchen stuff; and their fresh eggs, imported from France and Scotland. – Now, all these enormities might be remedied with a very little attention to the articles of police, or civil regulation; but the wise patriots of London have taken it into their heads, that all regulation is inconsistent with liberty; and that every man ought to live in his own way, without restraint – Nay, as there is not sense enough left among them, to be discomposed by the nuisance I have mentioned, they may, for aught I care, wallow in the mire of their own pollution.

8

And there's the other...

A TOURIST on Torremolinos
Artnik

I don't know if you've ever been to Torremolinos. If you holiday there, you're probably reading the wrong book. But even so, read on and be insulted. You deserve it.

I once had the misfortune of staying over a day in Torremolinos while passing through to Grenada. My God, it was Dante's seventh circle of hell. Picture the scene, if you will.

Row upon row of English-style pubs, overflowing with pile upon pile of sunburnt Brits. But only the very worst type of Brits abroad. Fat, sweating, topless, their poky legs jutting out of their shorts, their enormous bellies hanging over their belts. The tops of their bellies were bright red, and the rest of them milk-white.

I'm talking about the women as much as the men here. But what distinguished the men were the white or union-jack handkerchiefs with four knotted corners perched derisively on top of their shiny bald heads. The kids screamed at their feet, the mothers screamed at them to shut up, and all of them screamed at the Spaniard waiters or taxi drivers for not understanding them.

The only phrase these people bother to learn in Spanish is 'dos cervezas, por favor'. Not that they need it - everyone speaks English anyway.

You see, this is the REALLY depressing thing about Torremolinos. I don't resent these people for how they look, or how they speak, or what they know. But it's how little they try.

Let's have another look at these bars they hang around in. 'Alan's English Pub.' 'O'Malley's Irish Bar.' 'Yates's Costa Wine Lodge.' In these pubs you can guarantee draught English beer. They serve it in pint glasses. The people behind the bar, they not only speak English, they ARE English – they probably wouldn't understand a native if he asked them for directions out of this hell-hole. Christ, they even accept English currency.

And what are they showing on the big screens? English sporting events. The English Premiership. Even the English lower divisions – you see, the great thing is, there are no legal restrictions on how many games you can watch there, all day Saturday if you fancy it. And you can drink Stella or John Smiths with fellow Villa supporters, or fight them if they're Blues, and you never once have to remember you're in Spain.

So why exactly are they in Spain, if they could have done all this and stayed in England? Well, it's the 'bladdy

weather' presumably – it's hotter out in Spain, innit? Except that's the main cause of complaint. It's TOO bladdy hot for these peeling whales to sit out in the sun, and they do nothing but sweat and burn and moan, and get irritable headaches because they're dehydrating on all the pints of wife-beater they're knocking back.

So they stay indoors and pretend they're in their front room. Of course, the food's all greasy here, not like at home – but at least you can get proper pie 'n' mash or fish and chips at the canteen over the road next to the gift shop selling dirty postcards and replica England shirts. And for the final touch, open up your paper, check your missus isn't looking and get an eyeful of the Page 3 girl – all in the soar-away Sun, with 200,000 copies printed in Spain every day from May to September. And every page complaining about bloody foreigners coming over here and acting like they own the place.

A GERMAN (!) on the English in Marbella
Hubertus Erfurt

Last weekend I was in Marbella. It was so funny!! The best thing are these nouveau riche English people the place is packed with. Apart from the fact that my English is not perfect I have the feeling that my pronunciation is by far better than theirs. The most heard names were: Gary, Dave ('Dive'); Sharon, Jane and Tracy ('Try-say') and each of them drives either Bentley, Porsche, Mercedes ('Merc') or Jaguar ('Jag').

Many of them reminded me of Jeremy Clarkson from *Top Gear* a BBC motor programme or Bricktop the

London mobster in that wonderful film *Snatch* by Guy Ritchie. The guys are pleasant to talk to.

But coming to the girls one gets a different impression. The English girls appear to me to be almost clinicly disturbed. The looks are weird to start with: I cannot tell if it is courage or stylistic disorientation that they squeeze their hippo legs in stiletto Manolos combined with ultra short skirts. All of this topped with an almost invisible piercing of the belly button.

Their drinking habits are outrageous but their most irritating trait is their way of talking with a 50,000 megahertz voice that can make a long drink glass crack, combined with the thickest east London accent and the talking speed of a Gatling on full recoil.

They made me think about the chicken and egg conundrum: did these unnerving English girls cause the vast number of homosexual men found in England or was it all the gays that turned these girls into such ghastly parodies and caricatures of femininity.

No wonder these kind of English have such dreary sex lives. In short, it is because of the excessive abuse of alcohol by both genders. Shakespeare, the only true genius the English ever produced, summed it all up: 'Alcohol provokes the desire but takes away the performance.'

The biology of it is that under the influence of too much alcohol the man's normally high level of testosterone drops precipitously, whereas the woman's normally low level rises. What then happens is that the woman's natural inhibitions are removed, while the man's lack of them remains the same but his performance is abysmal.

What then occurs is a very Hobbesian type of sex: nasty, brutish and short. Hobbes was a very English philosopher.

163

There is a lot more to sex than sex

I hate it how men will tell you how beautiful and perfect you are. A week later you go his computer and see porn sites in the history. You look them up and they turn out to be the fake slutty women who have nothing better to do than post their naked asses online. When I confront him about this he tries to blame it on me, saying that I upset him or that I was such a bitch.'

Things Men Need to Know:

The reason our bras don't always match our underwear is because WE actually CHANGE our underwear.

The next time you and your buddies joke about armed women in combat, take a poll to see which of you successfully aim at the toilet bowl.

If we're watching football with you, it's not bonding. We're watching because of the butts.

If the truth hurts, ask us those ego-sensitive questions on your payday.

Whenever possible, please try to say whatever you have to say after the movie.

Please don't drive when you're not driving.

Our bedtime headaches are inversely proportional to the number of baths that you take.

If you were really looking for an honest answer you wouldn't ask in bed.

The next time you joke about female drivers, research the number of accidents caused by rubbernecking at miniskirts.

Stop telling us that most male strippers are gay: WE DON'T CARE!

Start parting and combing your hair to one side early in life: You'll never see the island coming.

Your contributions to your child should go above and beyond that semen you unselfishly sacrificed. Parenting does not end with conception.

Eye contact is best established above our shoulder level. We do not want sleazy underwear for Christmas presents. Money or jewellry is perfectly acceptable.

It is unacceptable to relieve yourself anywhere but the bathroom, when you do you aim straight and put the toilet lid down afterwards.

You can fall asleep without IT if you really try but, if you are not prepared to wait, please stay awake after IT. For a while anyway.

The weekend and sport on TV are not synonymous.

The correct answer to 'Do I look fat?' is never, ever 'Yes.'

Ditto for 'Is she prettier than me?'

Ordering for us is good. Telling us what we want is bad. Telling us not to wear revealing clothers is bad.

Don't flap the blankets after farting. Women learn not to eat food that causes flatulence, you do not even consider it. Flapping the blanket is no solution.

None of your ex-girlfriends was ever nicer, prettier, or better in bed.

Buying dinner does not equal foreplay.

Answering 'Who was that on the phone?' with 'Nobody' is never going to end that conversation.

Ditto for 'Whose lipstick is this?'

No means No. Yes means Yes. Silence could mean anything she feels like at that particular moment in time, and it could change without notice.

'Will you marry me?' is good. 'Let's move in together' is bad.
Never let her walk anywhere alone after 11pm.
Chivalry and feminism are NOT mutually exclusive.
Pick her up at the airport. Don't whine about it, just do it.
If you want to break up with her, break up with her. Don't
act like a complete jerk until she does it for you.
Don't tell her you love her if you don't.
Tell her you love her if you do. Often.
Remember Valentine's Day, and any 'anniversary' she so
names.
Don't try to change the way she dresses.
Her haircut is never bad.
The rules are never fair: accept this without question.

RETRO-MAN
Internet

**If everyone is thinking alike, then somebody isn't
thinking.** – General G.S.Patton
WHO!! RaRaRa!!
Ok folks, I have had it. I've taken all I can stand and I
can't stand no more. Every time my TV is on, all that can
be seen is effeminate men prancing about, redecorating
houses and talking about foreign concepts like 'style'
and 'feng shui'. Heterosexual, homosexual, bisexual,
trans-sexual, metrosexual, non-sexual; blue, green, and
purple-sexual.

Bogus definitions have taken over the world!
Real men of the world, stand up, scratch your a***,
belch, and yell 'ENOUGH!'

I hereby announce the start of a new offensive in the culture wars, *the Retrosexual movement.*

The RetroSexual Code:

A Retrosexual does not let neighbours screw up rooms in his house on national TV.

A Retrosexual, no matter what the women insists, PAYS FOR THE DATE.

A Retrosexual opens doors for a lady. Even for the ones that fit that term only because they are female.

A Retrosexual DEALS with IT. Be it a flat tire, break-in into your home, or a natural disaster, you DEAL WITH IT.

A Retrosexual not only eats red meat, he often hunts and kills it himself.

A Retrosexual doesn't worry about living to be 90. It's not how long you live, but how well. If you're 90 years old and still smoking cigars and drinking, I salute you.

A Retrosexual does not use more hair or skin products than a woman. Women have several supermarket aisles of stuff. Retrosexuals need one bathroom shelf (possibly 2 if you include shaving goods.)

A Retrosexual should know how to properly kill stuff (or people) if need be. This falls under the 'DEALING WITH IT' portion of The Code.

A Retrosexual watches no TV show with 'Queer' or 'Gay' in the title.

A Retrosexual should not give up excessive amounts of manliness for women. Some is inevitable, but major re-invention of yourself will only lead to you becoming a froo-froo little puss, and in the long run, she isn't worth it.

A Retrosexual is allowed to seek professional help for major mental stress such as drug/alcohol addiction, death of your entire family in a freak accident, favourite sports team being moved to a different city, or favourite dog expiring, etc. You are NOT allowed to see a shrink because Daddy didn't pay enough attention to you. Daddy was busy DEALING WITH IT. When you screwed up, he DEALT with you.

A Retrosexual will have at least one outfit in his wardrobe designed to conceal himself from prey.

A Retrosexual knows how to tie a Windsor knot when wearing a tie – and ONLY a Windsor knot.

A Retrosexual should have at least one good wound he can brag about getting.

A Retrosexual knows how to use a basic set of tools. If you can't hammer a nail, or drill a straight hole, practice in secret until you can – or be rightfully ridiculed for the wuss you be.

A Retrosexual knows that owning a gun is not a sign that your are riddled with fear, guns are TOOLS and are often essential to DEAL WITH IT. Plus it's just plain fun to shoot.

Crying. There are very few reason that a Retrosexual may cry, and none of them have to do with TV commercials, movies, or soap operas. Sports teams are sometimes a reason to cry, but the preferred method of release is swearing or throwing the remote control. Some reasons a Retrosexual can cry include (but are not limited to) death of a loved one, death of a pet (fish do NOT count as pets in this case), loss of a major body part.

A Retrosexual man's favourite movie isn't *Maid in Manhattan* (unless that refers to some foxy French maid sitting in a huge tub of brandy or whiskey), or *Divine Secrets of the Ya-Ya Sisterhood*. Acceptable ones may include any of the Dirty Harry or Nameless Drifter movies (Clint in his better days), *Rambo I* or II, the *Dirty Dozen*, The *Godfather* trilogy, *Scarface*, *The Road Warrior*, The *Die Hard* series, *Caddyshack*, *Rocky* I, II, or III, *Full Metal Jacket*, any James Bond Movie, *Raging Bull*, *Bullitt*, any Bruce Lee movie, *Apocalypse Now*, *Goodfellas*, *Reservoir Dogs*, *Fight Club*, etc .

A Retrosexual will have hobbies and habits his wife and mother do not understand, but that are essential to his manliness, in that they offset the acceptable manliness decline he suffers when married/engaged in a serious healthy relationship – i.e., hunting, boxing, shot putting, shooting, cigars, car maintenance.

A Retrosexual knows how to sharpen his own knives and kitchen utensils.

A Retrosexual man doesn't need a contract – a handshake is good enough. He will always stand by his word even if circumstances change or the other person deceived him.

A Retrosexual man doesn't immediately look to sue someone when he does something stupid and hurts himself. We understand that sometimes in the process of doing things we get hurt and we just DEAL WITH IT.

Retrosexual Tips for Women

Don't make us look pussywhipped or like you are the boss in front of our friends. This puts us in an uncomfortable position and we catch grief later about it from our friends. This is also how you get a guy's friends to turn against you and start suggesting he ditch you.

Don't get mad if you catch us looking at porn. We are with you and not these other girls. Most importantly just because we look at other girls does not mean we will cheat on you! Keep in mind women are into erotic stimulation as well. Romance Novels are the number one selling category of books and guys don't complain.

We can't read minds and men seldom think about the hidden meaning to words and actions. If you don't tell us what you are thinking or feeling don't expect us to figure it out. Men are as bad at taking hints as women are at giving them.

Your sudden change in emotions will confuse men. Understand we don't know what is going on inside your head most of the time. Often in these times neither do you.

Do not enter a conversation that you know nothing about, then get angry when you lose. This is one of the most annoying things ever. FACT: You're not always right!

If a guy treats you bad don't put up with it. As with human nature we will get away with whatever we can. Don't expect an asshole to change unless you are serious about leaving him.

Men want to be a part of your life and we want to know more about you. But don't expect us to remember every detail, person and drama you tell us about. A woman's life often has many situations and we enjoy knowing all of them as much as daytime soaps. Further, most guys are too nice to say you are boring the crap out of us. We start tuning you out after a certain amount of gossip.

Don't be so demanding of our time that you try to make us feel guilty when we want to do other things. There are parts of a guy's life that we enjoy doing without girls and you wouldn't be interested in anyway.

This DOESN'T mean we love you any less! Give us our space without giving us grief.

If you feel like straying, or if you're feeling bored with the guy, TELL HIM. Don't hide it, or try to suppress it by having cybersex with other people on the Internet... Think: if you tell him, he can try to give you more attention of whatever it is you think you need.

Almost all your guy friends are hoping to get in your pants. If you don't believe me tell them you have AIDS and are happy for their friendship in your time of need. Then see how many stick around. The point is your guy's jealousy about other men is justified.

Do not spend a lot of time getting dressed up on our account. Ninety-five percent of heterosexual guys could care less much less remember in a week what you were wearing. We like our girls to look good but the point of diminishing returns kicks in early.

Trying not to hurt our feelings by hoping we get the hint doesn't work. If you do not want to see or date us, not telling us is more confusing and painful than being upfront. You are not sparing our feelings by avoiding us, but making us feel worse.

Believe it or not guys enjoy it when girls do romantic things for us. We appreciate extra attention and gifts as much as you do. Few guys have experienced this. Go the extra distance and see if that doesn't warm a guy up to you.

If you hang out with other guys expect us to have a problem with it. These guys are trying to get into your pants and we know this. See an earlier tip for how to tell.

It's true, one way to a guys heart is through his stomach. Cooking can be very seductive to men.

Never let an ex-boyfriend meet your current unless want to make everyone very uncomfortable. Or want a fight.

If you have a problem with a guy's pets you might want to find a new man. Asking a guy to give up his animals will create long-term resentment.

If you have more problems than the guy you should hide them for as long as you can.

Guys don't enjoy meeting your parents. He is in bed with their daughter after all. Try to make doing so as painless as possible.

Looks do count, but they are not everything. If you look healthy and take care of yourself don't worry too much about your appearance. Otherwise your body might be running guys off.

Large breasts are enjoyable but are seldom the deciding factor in girls we date. Don't worry about it so much.

Don't talk about your ex and especially sex you have had with other men. We don't want to hear about other guys who have had you. It is OK to talk about sex and what you like but don't include names, time or places.

Never tell a guy you have had better sex, at least not if you want to have sex with him again.

Just because you don't like seeing yourself in the mirror, doesn't mean your man sees the same flaws you see. Leave the lights ON.

PETER HITCHENS on culture wars:
Mail on Sunday

I like to think that I've won a few victories in the war of ideas about morality and culture. Isn't every responsible parent revolted by the sexual pollution which infests magazines such as *Sugar*, aimed, for heaven's sake, at children?

How we get so steamed up about paedophilia but are so unsteamed by this sexualisation of the young I cannot understand.

Telling children about sex and equipping them for it with condoms and abortion pills is always justified, by the weirdos who support it, on the grounds it will reduce teen pregnancy and disease.

But since the new frankness began thirty-five years ago, teen pregnancy and sexual disease have never ceased to increase.

Isn't it a kind of madness to carry on with such an obvious failure? Yet publishers, civil servants, ministers and supposed experts continue to support it.

Loos on Beck's dongle
Summer of George: JustRamIt.co.uk

But this Loos woman...she can pack it right in. I hear she has made £850,000 from this deal...and had numerous offers for jobs on the television from it all. But she has been at great pains to stress that all the fame and fortune are not at all what she is interested in. She felt she must speak out because she was 'tired of living a lie', which was why she asked Max Clifford to help her tell the truth.

Now Miss Loos, listen very carefully: 'You are a transparent gold-digging Liar and a hopeless publicity whore.' But I have to say I was deeply upset that Beckham did not sue you as I was waiting to see exactly what it was regarding his 'manhood' that you could reveal to prove your case.

Was a cowbell attached, is it made of polystyrene?... can it place an in-swinging corner right onto the head of the

173

centre back in the six yard box? Sadly we shall never know.

But this whole sorry escapade has once again revealed how pathetically childish we are as a nation regarding Sex. Hee hee. People having sex...with their computer screen.

Now I am far from a prude...and at least Porn is honest. Look: people, naked, shagging...that's it. Now if you are some loopy fetishist I don't want to know, keep me out of it, you maniac, with your erotic obsession over cutlery or Nesquik. But that's porn in its broad strokes: people humping away for other people to masturbate over. Oh yeah, we'll put the 'it's a love making aid' defence to one side and laugh at it later.

But porn isn't good enough for the British Public, we need softcore titillation from our national newspapers all the time, and ribald jaunty gossip about celebrity infidelities. Because we all have such moribund empty lives. Have you read the letters pages of a tabloid recently?

It would appear that everyone in Britain is now sleeping with either their brother, father-in-law, next door neighbour, best friend's beau or the photocopier repairman. I read one yesterday...

And no word of a lie it was from some woman asking advice regarding the fact her husband had bought her a strap-on dildo and wanted her to poke him up the a***.

She was uncertain what to do and wanted the agony aunt's advice. And she got it...the advice I mean. What the newspaper should have done is track these people down and shame them publicly with a fourteen-page photo spread.

You want advice on such a matter. Well here's a tip: don't write to a national newspaper asking for it, as one day you may get just get the 14-page photo spread you deserve.

And do, please for all our sakes, grow up.

Sex-Text Maniacs Rants
Internet

I want gritty violence n sex on TV, but put it on at 11pm, not in soaps and prime-time dramas! That's family time. – Benito, Plymouth.

Don't let Cor St have gays kissing, think of families viewing. Aggie ur a gr8 paper, always cheeky sumtimes controversial. Dnt b hypocritical - sum peeps r gay, so wot? d, brum IF THEY SHOW GAY MALE SEX THEN THEY SHOULD SHOW LESBIANS MORE 2.

I'm a young teenager who recently cum out as gay. Ur comments make it sound like a disease. Sex is sex whether straight or gay! Mark WHAT'S ALL THE FUSS ABOUT THE GAY KISS IN CORONATION STREET? MEN HAVE BEEN KISSING OTHER BLOKES 4 YEARS IN MANCHESTER! FITZ EastEnders not up for best soap Bafta? The shock of it! The Bafta people have finally realised what depressing crap it is! G.H, Hants I am a black guy born & bred here.

This country is not racist. It's the pc sticking its nose in, telling us what 2 say & what 2 think. B****cks.

Curtis I dnt care wat ne1 finks, on St George's day I'm walking da streets draped in a St George's cross, showin off my England tattoo across my stomach! matt PLEASE CONFIRM ST GEORGE'S DAY IS APRIL 1st. GAZ Britain records highest number of uk workers in employment. Great, that means more income tax, less benefits paid out. so where's the money going, Tony and Gordon?

WHEN IS ROBIN HOOD REAPPEARING TO SAVE US FROM THE GOVERNMENT?

So now late trains are the PASSENGERS' fault?! Train bosses whistling out of the wrong end – again.

The best way to broadcast your inflated ego
Internet

These days every second person seems to have personalised ('cherished') number plates. The only plus to this is that you can spot self-centred morons as far as your eye can see. There are two forms of plates that match two forms of losers. Firstly there is the ones that have your initials e.g.'JF-898' or 'DH-007' – the latter conveys the meaning 'Dick Head, and I think I am something spectacular like a James Bond wannabe'.

I'd like to use this forum as a means of communicating a simple message to owners of such plates:
NOBODY GIVES A S**T IN HELL WHAT YOUR INITIALS ARE!!

I can't understand the benefit of paying money so people on the road know the first letters of your name. Or is it so when you go to your car you can see the plates as an aid to remembering your own name? It wouldn't surprise me as you obviously have the mentality of a Baboon's scrotum. Why not have 'I love myself' tattooed on your forehead or clone yourself so you can get freaky with yourself.

Perhaps I'm missing the point...but that's almost impossible. Maybe it's so you can be easily identified by your worthless friends so they can do something amazing in a response to spotting you like wave or honk their horn... I know that would make MY day.

The worst thing is that it costs about £200 to do this. If

I was stupid enough to spend £200 on a bunch of letters that mean only something to myself, I would not want to be identified. I'd be embarrassed, like walking out of a whorehouse and bumping into my kindergarten teacher. What must people who own these plates be like? They obviously think they're important enough to care what their initials are, but if they WERE important we'd already KNOW their initials. Here's a tip: Spend the money on something worthwhile that doesn't include broadcasting the fact that you're an idiot and tremendously proud of it.

The other type of plates is the ones that attempt to say a word but it's normally displayed with the grammatical stylings of a 4 year old child with Parkinson's disease. Words like 'Stolen' or 'Bachelor' or 'W***er'. Then because there is a large contingent of like-minded asshole people those words get taken so they change them to 'St0ln' 'Bachala' or 'Wanka'.

Some plates can even be sold for thousands just to get a name for your car that amuses yourself repeatedly. You're like a goldfish that swims around and sees a new plant every two seconds but it's the same plant. Surely the idea of a word on your number plate gets old...or do you share more similarities with memory-deficient animals than we understand? I would suggest that is the only answer.

So if you're considering personalised number plates, think long and hard about euthanasia first. People won't miss you, if they cared enough about you then you wouldn't have to tell them your initials or that you're a 'HRNYBACHLA'.

You're going to get a huge shock one day when you realise the world is bigger than yourself. I hope you wet your pants and torture yourself with questions like why you wasted your life being an idiot and thinking you were anything special.

Kindly perish away with the slow decay of time in isolation looking at yourself in a mirror. It's a win/win situation.

Get off your fat a***
Fat People

Scientists are on the verge of discovering the world's first 'fat' pill, which they're hoping will improve our waistlines and overall well being. While the manufacturers say it could be more than four years until it's available, they're calling for volunteers to take part in an extensive trial in an effort to determine its safety and effectiveness.

Great, another medical marvel that will cheat lazy fat asses into fitness... Could be more than 4 years? I can show you a way to be thin even before it comes out.

Here are the 5 easy steps... the REAL answers to obesity:

1. Get off your fat ass. No diet will work if you sit on the couch all day. It's sitting still that's made you fat... move your flabby thunder thighs before it's too late. Stop watching garbage like Oprah Winfrey, she won't empower you and she's still fat anyway.

2. Stop eating! How many fat Ethiopians do you see? Go over there for a holiday and if you don't lose the weight, they'll eat you and put you out of your misery. Why not solve your problem and theirs all in one go, I bet you'd be tasty with some hot sauce.

3. Make friends. Food is not your friend. Like 88% of

fatties have an emotional attachment. You love food but I have news for you. Food doesn't love you! Food hates you, after all look what it's done to you: food made you fat so stop being friends with it.

4. Stop pointing the finger. All you lard burgers love to blame other people or genetic predispositions. You don't have fat genes and even if it runs in your family, what is blaming that going to do for your 19 chins? Take responsibility for what you've done to yourself, Chubs.

5. Read women's magazines. Nothing will make you realise how enormous you are than looking at Calista Flockhart's ribs poking from underneath her blouse. Fair enough she's an idiot but she's got more friends than you and she's not going to die at 40. So many women go on TV saying 'wow, look at me I lost a million pounds and I still look great'. Correction, you look better but you're still a butterball. You went from elephant to hippo... you're on the track but the work's not over yet. I'm not a fan of anorexics, but they're good role models for fat people. Fat people need to wake up and smell the lean cuisine. People aren't going to do it for you, lazy bastards. And if you won't follow these steps then you must do the following:

Stop opening plus size clothing stores that make fat people feel comfortable and give them no reason to unclog the KFC from their arteries.

Stop going to the beach because it makes people want to vomit. Also sun-bathers don't take too kindly to having the beach all shaded up by your fat bum that blocks the sun.

Don't have children. If you've failed in the skinny stakes at least don't raise children to be tormented failures like yourself. Nobody likes a fat kid, and they're never 'cute' despite what people say.

That's it, a simple solution to a simple problem.

ENJOY!

KEITH AITKEN: Assorted rants
Daily Express

Full marks to the *Express*'s David Robson for highlighting the noise pollution caused by the incessant drum-driven music TV's condescending bosses think we plebs need to help us concentrate. But what about drivers whose car stereos belt out dance music at a zillion decibels?

We've rightly outlawed motorists with cell phones clamped to their ears, surely it's every bit as distracting to drive in a mobile nightclub?

I see my local branch of IKEA is claiming that someone has nicked £15,000-worth of furniture. If there is eventually a conviction, I hope the court exercises leniency. The poor dope's already facing a life sentence when he tries to assemble the stuff.

Our councillor, Brian Meek, is also a columnist in *The Herald* of Glasgow. This week Brian warned readers against votes for 16-year-olds: 'At 16 I would have been unable to make any political judgment.' Right, Brian. And how old were you when you agreed to become an advisor to Michael Forsyth?

The sort of people who always know better than the courts are outraged that The Who should be back on stage for the first time since Pete Townsend's caution for looking at child porn on the Internet. Me, I'm just outraged that a band with neither Keith Moon nor John Entwistle in it would pretend to be The Who.

Modern Manners
Internet Posting

Post by Jason: This irritates the hell of me, to see a man or even worse women shoving a Gregg's pasty or a McDonalds' burger into there mouth as they walk in the street. This has to stop.
PLEASE LET IT STOP NOW!
It really turns my stomach and I want to smack these people or maybe educate them that sitting down, taking time out to enjoy your food is important and results in a more aesthetically pleasing environment for me!

Riposte by Lizzieboreden: Personally I would rather see someone eat a roast dinner in the street than listen to any more boring f****rs yakking on their mobiles.

I don't object to mobiles – in fact the woman on the train next to me yesterday was having a fantastically interesting row and the whole carriage was gripped, soap opera style – it's just people saying such dull things, so loudly.

And please answer the question as to why it is worse to see a woman eating in the street? Is it unladylike to scoff down a pork pie between business engagements? Should she not be in the street but at home cooking your dinner? Do you object to woman eating full stop and thus fancy Posh? I think we should be told.

I often eat in the street, but not bananas or sausages as then builders make comments.

WHEN ADVERTISEMENTS CROSS THE LINE
Consumer Watch

Watching ads on TV is akin to listening to an album by Kylie Minogue... it sucks. Even worse is watching a TV show ABOUT ads. Even the 'world's best ads still blow because they are ADS!

As long as I can remember, sex has been used to sell anything and everything. I give credit where credit is due to make breakfast cereal or some other obscure item somehow related to sex is beyond my feeble comprehension.

Sex is arguably the most powerful tool to selling products, but where do we draw the line? I have some suggestions:

Diabetes: Recently there has been a television add that uses sex to sell a little machine that tests your blood via a prick on your finger to see how close you are to dead. The add goes like 'I do it in the morning, I do it twice a day, I do it at work, I do it with my father... etc, etc.'. If there was ever an antidote to Viagra, that would have to be it. That would send noodles limp all around the globe.

Food Ads: I saw a Jerry Springer show one time where these sick bastards were getting naked and covering themselves in food. Subsequently I stopped eating for 6 months and nearly died of malnutrition. I still look at creamed corn suspiciously.

Sex ads: Viagra and Viagra ads should be banned. If you're too old and wrinkly to crack a wood then nature's telling you that you're disgusting and you'll only ever have sex if the woman is able to pretend you're someone else.

There's this ad on TV which is just about this lame guy on some stupid American TV drama. It goes: 'He's sexy, he's wild, which ever way you look at him he's fantastic to watch.' Something like that. I bet the guy paid for it himself. He's a sellout Australian who went to America and picked up an American accent in 3.4 seconds.

Car ads: If I see that seizure inducting Kia Rio ad again I'm going to snap. Some dumb bimbo stands in front of a bowl of keys like the whore she is, then looks at the guy she wants to sex and he mouths out the word 'Kia'. So she completely looks past a set of keys that say Kia and picks up a pair belonging to this guy with giant eyebrows. I hope she gets pregnant and dies in labour.

Tampons ads: Tampons are about a sexy as a gangrene infested nut sack. They repeatedly use commercials featuring some dense guy who tries to say something coherent yet manages to degrade the male race by being excessively muscular yet feminine and dense at the same time. I'm alluding to that ad where the guy thinks slim tampons mean you've lost weight or something. Tampons are gross.

So use your collective purchasing powers to boycott any product you'd not like to think about as you're about to get on the job. Together we can make the television free from things that turn a Penelope Cruz into a Margaret Thatcher.

An incomplete day in the life of a Ranter
Mr InsultMonger: JustRamIt.co.uk

7:30am – Goddamn alarm clock! Why can't clocks have ring tones? Why does it have to sound so utterly monotonous? Why not start the day with a little energising Wagner? Soon we'll have a chirpy American chick saying

'Rise and shine! You'll soon smell the Nescafe Gold Brand coffee available from Asda, a wholly-owned Wal-Mart subsidiary, at only £1.99 a jar. Your clock's built-in GPS has detected an Asda store only 4.7 kilometres from you! Have a nice day!' Why? Why? Why? Hmmm?

7:32am – And why do I always tip over the ashtray when fumbling for a refreshing Marlboro in the morning? Why hasn't someone invented ash-less cigarettes? Hmmm? Hmmm? I'll tell you why! It's because the tobacco companies are in league with the carpet cleaning detergents manufacturers, that's why!

7:44am – Your whole life is just a tiny cog in some giant corporation's buck-spinning wheel. And worse, it's a US corporation. Just like this toaster, I'll bet. Why does the butter always melt in it? Why hasn't someone invented butter that is resistant to heat? You can bet your life it's because some giant US corporation wants to evaporate half the global butter supply in toasters. Yeah, you could say 'You should butter your bread after you toast it.' But I'm not having some giant US corporation telling me how to make toast!

8:07am – Oh, for f**k's sake! Why does your finger always break through the toilet paper? Jesus! It gets under your fingernails and everything! Surely, someone should be sued over this.

8:14am – Oh, for double f**k's sake!! Why do you have to be stark naked and in the shower before you realise you forgot to turn the hot water immersion on? Have you ever tried wet-shaving with cold water? It's like pulling each hair out with a pliers.

8:32am – The same old s**t on the BBC news. Talking hairdos, exchanging pre-scripted banter, in-between showing pics of some British soldier's wife with new-born baby in arms (mysteriously black) missing her man who is busy beating The United Colours of Crapola out of some unfortunate Iraqi prisoner of unlawful occupation, while avoiding coverage of said Geneva Convention violations. Amazing! This PR-network for pro-British spin hails itself as a beacon of probity! That's like Michael Jackson and his Neverland Children's playground. Not that the Yank networks are any better. CBS turned the murders, rapes, and assorted human rights violations by American solders in an Iraqi prison into a story of the heroism of Private Grady, who blew the whistle on the shenanigans. Gee, instead of seeing the Yanks for the murdering scum they are, we got to see them as heroes – again!

8:32am – I'm off back to bed.

The only real laughter comes from despair.
Groucho Marx, The Groucho Letters